The Long White Cloud

The Maori speak of a land that the Polynesian demi-god Maui fished from the sea.

This land was called Aotearoa – New Zealand.

By Kristen Faber

ISBN-13: 978-1508647652
ISBN-10: 1508647658

Cover design by Robin Lindman

Dedication

Chad, my best friend and husband,
From the first dream of living in New Zealand
To the last period on the paper,
You have been with me every step of the way.

Damon, Maddie and Elena
You have filled my life with adventure and awe.

Ruth and Russell
Val and Stew
Theresa and Ian
Thank you for sharing your country, your passions and your love with me.
You will always be in my heart.

Table of Contents

Preface

My dirty blonde braids bounced against my back as I skipped down the street pulling my squeaky red wagon. Dad and I had loaded it full of the pumpkins we spent all summer growing together. I stopped at every house on my street and rang the doorbell. When someone answered the door, I stretched my eight-year-old body as tall as I could and asked, "Do you want to buy a pumpkin to support my missionary friend in Brazil?" It didn't take long to sell them all. I ran home, the money clutched tight in my fist. Perched on the front step I counted it. Eight dollars and twenty-seven cents. It was soooo much! Excitedly I wrote my friend, Reverend Hocking, a letter and told him I wanted the money to go to help the church in São Paulo, Brazil.

That night my mind wandered as I lay on my bed. The canopy bed was my ship to far off places. The light blue canopy was the wide open sky above me, full of possibility. The blue carpet was the sea. Sometimes it was filled with waves and sea monsters and other days it was calm and invited a good adventure. In charge of my ship and my destiny, I read biographies about pioneers, adventurers and missionaries. I lay there dreaming about what it was like to live in another country.

At church I was exposed to "Missionary Week" once a year. I stared at the screen as the slide projector beamed photos of jungles and big cities. Africans dressed in bright clothes with large white smiles and Indians in their saris and a distinctive red dot on their forehead filled the screen with color. A missionary family would stand on stage to sing a song in a foreign language. After service, as my parents visited, I went out to the lobby where tables were lined up—one for each missionary. The missionaries typically wore a costume from the country they lived in. They stood by their tables that were covered with things I had never seen before. Necklaces, toys, baskets, mementos and rattles made from gourds. One time when my friends and I were hanging around asking questions, the missionary reached behind his display and pulled out a snakeskin. He had us stand in a line, shoulder to shoulder as he slowly unrolled the skin. When he got to me a shiver ran down my spine as I clutched the dry, scaly skin. Soon the missionary was telling us stories about snakes in the jungle. That night the carpet around my ship became an angry sea swirling with crocodiles and reptiles.

My parents had a love for travel that they instilled in me early on. In preparation for the yearly family vacation, the kitchen table would be filled for weeks with AAA guides and notepads of blue graph paper. My dad made lists. He paced around the house muttering about the schedule and how to see every site along the way. Road maps for each state lay on top of everything with routes highlighted and notes scribbled in the margin. My dad pulled off the best family trips without the aid of a computer. The night before the big take-off he would lower the car top carrier onto the roof and begin to pack it full of sleeping bags, foam cushions and a tent. The next morning when nothing more could be squeezed into the car, we loaded in and waved goodbye. We typically made it to the corner before someone remembered that they had forgotten something. Around the block we would go, pull back into our driveway, and Mom would run in the house only to reappear a moment later with the ever-so-important item in her hand. This routine typically happened three to four times before everyone was satisfied that we had everything. By that time I was hunched low in my seat so the neighbors couldn't identify me as part of the family circus. On one particular trip I read nineteen Nancy Drew books. My mom was so furious when I pulled my eyes from the page only long enough to look out the window and say "Yeah… it is a big hole. I can see why they call it the Grand Canyon." Somewhere along the way, my dad got ahold of a book about camping America for free. The first night that we tried one of these campgrounds we pulled into our site in our typical style. It was 11:00. The sun had set hours ago and only the headlights of our van illuminated our little circus as we set up the tent. Exhausted, we fell asleep only to be wildly awakened at two in the morning by a train flying by just ten feet from our tent. We didn't use any more free campsites.

By the time I graduated from high school I had visited forty-nine of the fifty states as well as Canada and Mexico. In college I did a summer overseas study program where I wandered the streets of Italy and England. I was hooked—there were so many places to see and things to experience.

And then I fell in love. Suddenly all my dreams and plans began to revolve around this amazing man. He had spent a summer in Mali, Africa helping a friend on an irrigation project. They helped the locals provide water to grow crops in the Sahara desert. Chad and I got married and moved to Detroit so that he could complete his medical training. The five years we lived in Detroit were my first experience in a different culture. We still lived in Michigan, but this was a different world than I had grown up in. I soon had our first baby, a little boy we named Damon. I was grown up now. My mom took down the canopy bed and redid the room I grew up in. The books were packed in boxes and stacked in the basement. We had medical school and residency to concentrate on. Soon we added Maddie to our family and then a few years later Elena came. Life was full and busy, but thoughts of far off places continued to tickle our dreams.

Finally the medical training was done. We decided to volunteer for two months in West Africa before work began. Carolyn Kempton Memorial Hospital was located deep in the heart of Togo. People thought we were a bit crazy for taking a four-year-old, two-year-old and four-month-old to the wilds of Africa. The experience only deepened our love for people and cultures around the world.

We settled into life in Midwest America raising our little family and paying off medical school loans. Life was good. A few months before 9/11 Chad joined the Army Reserves. The attack on the towers in the fall of 2001 changed life in America forever. Deployment to Afghanistan added another layer of skills to his resume.

One day while we were sitting in our average middle-class home we realized that the kids were growing up and we were getting stuck in a rut. We were at a crossroads and we needed to choose a path. We had always wanted to live overseas and had been pursuing option after option. But nothing quite fit. That's when we started hearing about locum tenens agencies. Offices and hospitals in America and throughout the world who are in need of medical professionals advertise through these agencies. We began working with a company and looking through the lists of open positions. Some places were crossed out and others circled. We had never considered New Zealand because it wasn't exotic enough—they are a British Commonwealth country, speak English and just didn't seem to pull at us as other countries did. But New Zealand had many cities in need and so we finally settled on a particular city. We knew we needed to leave, to give our dreams a try, or we never would. So we signed on the dotted line and began our preparations.

For us this was a "do or die" moment. It was a new path—we had committed to one year, but we knew that there would be no returning to our previous way of life. We sold the house our children knew as "home." I began to sort through things. It is good to clean away the clutter, and the feeling of freedom was euphoric. But some things were hard to let go of. I had so many friends and acquaintances come up to me and say, "I could never do what you are doing. I would love to purge and downsize and get rid of stuff, but I just can't." I wanted to reply "You have no idea how hard this is. I love my things and I have many memories and sentiments attached to certain items. And besides, I just think some of it is pretty." I came to a point where I had to wrestle with what is most important to me in life. Is it my things? Are these possessions what I want to dictate my future decisions and experiences in life? Only time would tell if it was worth it to give up my middle class, suburban, American life.

After the decisions had been made and our things given away or put into storage, I sat there on my empty front porch. The friends who had helped us so faithfully were now gone. Tomorrow I would be getting on a plane with Chad and our three kids to face the unknown.

The Beginning

Every story has a beginning and an end. For me that magical place was Auckland, New Zealand. There actually was a "prequel" to my story: the decision to leave, selling or storing all our worldly possessions, explaining to family and friends our plan while trying not to appear crazy or out of our minds and ultimately packing up two suitcases per person and departing.

We said our tearful yet excited "goodbyes" in Grand Rapids, Michigan, boarded an airplane and set off for the adventure of our lives. The adventure itself was well underway by this point. The door to the plane opened and we stepped out nervous, tired, enthusiastic and naive. Half the world away, separated by continents and oceans, was a new country and a new life. A large mural in the Auckland airport expressed my feelings:

"Every flyer who ventures across oceans to distant lands
is a potential explorer; in his or her breast
burns the same fire
that urged adventurers of old
to set forth in their sailing-ships
for foreign lands."[1]
Jean Batten
Alone in the Sky
1979

Just as New Zealand brought out the adventurer in aviator Jean Batten, New Zealand would bring a sense of adventure to my family as well as any person who visits this country.

We had twenty-four jet-lagged, bleary-eyed hours to see Auckland before hitting the road. We stuck close to our downtown hotel during the day, delighted to find a familiar Chicago feel to the town along with a distinct modern European flair. We ambled down alleys finding boutiques and cafes and wandered in and out of little shops. Our greatest delight was the warm welcome to New Zealand that we received from the locals.

Day two found us cramming fourteen suitcases, five carry-ons and five people into a rented minivan. With two bike boxes strapped to the top of the vehicle, we looked and felt a bit like the Beverly Hillbillies!

New Zealand

When I mentioned to friends that we were moving to New Zealand, a far-off dreamy look often appeared in their eyes. Visions of rolling hills dotted with sheep, rivers twisting through the landscape and snow-capped mountains begging to be climbed filled their minds. This idyllic picture of New Zealand is true. But on the other hand, comments about Aboriginals, kangaroos and hobbits wandering the country aren't!

New Zealand is made up of two small islands. The square mileage is just larger than my home state of Michigan and actually closer to the size of Colorado. You cannot see Australia across the Tasman Sea. In fact, Australia is a friendly neighbor with a healthy rivalry in all things from Rugby to Vegemite.

The original name of New Zealand, Aotearoa, comes from a popular mythological Maori story. After a long ocean voyage, the explorer Kupe was nearing land. An unusually long white cloud hovered over it. He pointed and exclaimed to his wife, "Surely this is a point of land." Hine-te-aparangi, his wife, called out, "He ao! He ao!" (A cloud! A cloud!) Kupe decided to name the new land after his wife's greeting and the cloud that welcomed them.

Now four million people inhabit the country with over half the population living in the three largest cities: Auckland, Wellington and Christchurch. This leaves the majority of the land gloriously vacant, begging exploration.

My husband, Chad, had a fabulous outlook on the country. "It's unbelievably beautiful. Once you get a look at it the subject is barely even debatable—not really, unless you're just a grinch opposed to the idea that anyone should ever be happy and that puppies are soft and cuddly. I find it hard to put into words. It borders on the ridiculous. You almost get tired of hearing yourself say 'Holy cow, that's gorgeous!' Surely there must be somewhere in the world that is scenically challenged because New Zealand got more than its share.

"Hills are the major topographical feature; there is little flat to the land at all. Much of it is used for farming and the hills are not spared from grazing. This leads to an interesting impression that isn't immediately apparent upon taking in the beauty (indeed, it's a major factor in the beauty): everything, even the most remote mountains and steepest hills (sparing only sheer cliffs), has the appearance of newly manicured lawns. And it is fairly literally that. Cows get what little level ground there is, sheep help with that and chew the hillsides, while goats are seen picking their way along steep, craggy and scree-strewn mountainsides. Driving through the roughest terrain, the view is rolling hills with mown grass and no weeds. Rocky outcroppings and tall ornamental plants growing wild add to the natural beauty, while small meandering streams are absolutely everywhere. Just when you think you can't see a prettier scene, you round a bend and between two of these mind-bogglingly beautiful hills is a view of the sea. I think this must be the birthplace of the postcard.

"And some mundane reaction like 'Holy cow that's gorgeous!' just doesn't cut it. Not in New Zealand. This calls for more than your run-of-the-mill compliment. I seem to recall David out of the Bible gyrating half-naked in the streets to celebrate one particularly momentous event. Now that's more like it! His wife thought his reaction was ridiculous, but how does one underline something really, really awesome? How about singing at the top of your lungs or dancing naked... All of which explains why I think that my son's, Damon's, first reaction was really a pretty good one. After a couple hours of taking in your fill of beauty, beauty and then another heaping helping of more gorgeous beauty, you've got to let it out somehow."

Mixed with the beauty is a sense of peacefulness. It's hard to live in such a serene place and not be affected. The Global Peace Index of 2012 placed New Zealand as the second most peaceful place to live in the world. That says a lot. I felt it in the people around me. The whole country gave me a home-towny safe feeling that wiped away the little bit of tension that I never knew I had.

Several months later my daughter, Maddie, and I were driving home from a day of appointments and shopping in the next town over. The sun had just set. We were creeping around the curves in the dark, slowly making our way home, enjoying the quiet. The next bend revealed a car pulled onto the shoulder and the silhouette of a large man with curly wild hair standing next to the car. Without a second thought I pulled up and asked if he needed help. His car was broken and he needed a ride into town. He climbed in the back seat and as I pulled onto the road, I sucked in my breath, realizing what I had just done. I would never do that in America. A woman and her daughter, in the dark on desolate roads forty minutes from home should never pick up a male hitchhiker. But I did and I was safe. That is the kind of world I want to live in. One where it is safe to help a stranger. Where we know that we will be helped when we need it because other people do not fear us. That is the sort of country New Zealand is.

The Right or Wrong Side of the Road?

With the van packed to the gills and everyone settled into a nook, Chad got behind the wheel. We took a deep breath, mentally focused and slowly pulled onto the left side of the road. Everything felt backwards and mixed up for about the first hour until we settled into "driving on the wrong side of the road." At each corner I would grab the seat and hold my breath as we looked back and forth twenty times to be sure no cars were going to plow into us from any direction.

Our eight-hour journey from Auckland to Wairoa was beautiful. The countryside is what New Zealand is known for, and every moment spent in the car proved that. Cows grazing in fields, sheep dotting the landscape—postcard perfect. We took our time as if on our honeymoon winding through little towns and stopping for burgers at lunch (bewildered by the beets piled on top), delighted at all things new.

The first five hours of the trip passed uneventfully. We were in love with this new country—enjoying our first day of partnership. We noticed that we were down to half a tank of gas. No worries, every little town seemed to have a gas station. Not thinking, we continued on, and on and on. The gentle winding roads of the interior began to change into sharp twists with very exposed cliffs as we turned up and down steep, beautiful mountains. All this while driving on the left side of the road!

It was June, the middle of winter in New Zealand, and we had not taken into account the shortness of the days. Two days earlier we had been in Michigan where we enjoyed long days stretching into the night. The sun did a glorious dip below the horizon as our gas gage did the same. Chad and I began to discuss the sudden disappearance of gas stations while the kids began to complain of nausea from the curves. Panicked, we yelled at them to roll down the window as our oldest, Damon, proceeded to cough up his dinner in spectacular style at fifty miles per hour around a steep mountain bend. We pulled over at the first possible moment to settle our nerves. Our brains were fried and our bodies tired. Only wanting a warm meal and cozy bed, we focused our attention back on the drive ahead. We got a good laugh at the side of the van. It looked like a bird, with airline food in its belly, had hit our car at terminal velocity.

It was now dark outside. We loaded back into the van. The gas light blinked on. We were exhausted. Every hairpin turn we crept around dashed our hopes of a gas station. I gripped the car door, certain each curve would bring sudden death by plummeting off the side of a mountain. Prayers whispered in pure fear carried us down the road. Suddenly, we found ourselves in the middle of a small town.

That's how our jet-lagged family of five arrived on fumes, in the dark, with dinner splattered across the side of the van, to our new home town of Wairoa.

First Impressions

It was only 6:30 in the evening but darkness and silence hung over the little town. We were exhausted and hungry with no idea where to go. No instructions, no cell phone, no map. We found the hospital where my husband would be working, but they couldn't get ahold of anyone to tell us where our house was or to let us in. They seemed to know less about us than we did of them, so they sent us to "Funky Foods" (seriously, that's really the name!)—the only place in town still open to get a bite to eat. Somebody got ahold of someone who found us and took us to our new home. I focused on the house by the headlights as we pulled up. I whispered with a shaky voice to my husband, "We're going to live in a single wide mobile home." I don't know what my expectations were, but a mobile home was not one of them. We were shown in and handed the keys. All I wanted to do was sit down and cry. The wallpaper was from the Sixties, the worn carpet from the Seventies, the curtains didn't match and were from the Eighties. The cold water in the bathroom didn't work, the toilet paper holder was falling off the wall and the refrigerator and drawers were filled with half consumed food. I pulled myself together—

more for the kids than for myself. We brought in the luggage and got everyone into bed. Oh, did I mention that it was winter and homes in New Zealand don't have central heat? We started the wood burning stoves but it took two days before a long sigh didn't end in a frosty cloud hanging in the air.

Life always looks brighter after a good night of sleep. It turned out we didn't live in a mobile home. The house was cute with a yard reminding me of the Garden of Eden. My mouth began to water as I wandered around looking at the bounty. An orange tree, two mandarin trees, a grapefruit tree, a macadamia nut tree, a lemon tree, grapevines and a garden. Adam and Eve could not have been happier than I as I dreamed of the harvest these plants would bring.

Typical of New Zealand architecture, the house was wood-sided and painted white. It was quite likable in the morning sun, already beginning to feel like home. In the year to come I wandered through towns and neighborhoods and learned that residential architecture has a lot of charm and warmth.

Two of the main styles of homes originated in England. *Bay Villas* have a Victorian feel, boast a gabled roof, detailed fretwork around a veranda and a bay window in the front. Soft-colored exteriors work in harmony with flower gardens within the white picket fences. Small and charming, I dreamed of sitting in a wicker rocking chair while sipping lemonade on these front porches.

The *Craftsman* style homes are more boxy. Exposed rafters and thick square columns support the low-pitched roofs creating a long, wide porch. The earthy hues of the paint with stained glass windows feel warm and comfortable. A large chimney with smoke curling up speaks of warmth within on chilly days.

<u>Wairoa</u>

"Kia Ora" (kee-ora) greets visitors on a huge billboard as they drive into Wairoa. The Maori phrase means "welcome" and can be heard from locals as they greet one another with a hongi, the traditional Maori greeting of pressing nose-to-nose and forehead-to-forehead.

The Wairoa River begins west of Gisborne, snaking its way sixty-five kilometers to reach the heart of Wairoa where it finds its release in Hawkes Bay on the East coast of New Zealand. *Te Wairoa Hōpūpū Hōnengenenge Mātangi Rau* is what the Maori called the river. It means long, bubbling, swirling, uneven waters. The river runs through town under a bridge connecting downtown and North Clive areas.

Wairoa had its heyday in the fifties. Older folks in town would get a dreamy, far-off look in their eyes as they reminisced about attending movies in the now closed theater, or swirling girls around the dance floor and foxtrotting the night away in one of the three dance halls that have vanished just as the memories too will fade away.

The main industries in town are ranching in the gorgeous hills surrounding the city and the abattoir. I just loved the way the town folk would say the word "abattoir." It rolled off their tongues with a thick accent making everything sound romantic. In reality it is a fancy word for the meatworks, or more simply put, the slaughterhouse. The abattoir was tucked away on the other side of the river and I forgot about it except on hot, heavy days when the air hung thick with the stench of fresh meat and blood floating into town. Some of the old-timers I knew would stop me on the street and tell stories of the days when offal was thrown into the river and sharks came upstream from the ocean, into fresh water, to devour the dead animals.

A few incidents have put Wairoa on the map. Cyclone Bola in 1988 dumped more rain than anyone could remember in a short three-day period. Landslides, mudslides and floods devastated the community. Twenty years later my friends still clearly remember those days. I sat in their living rooms looking through old photographs of the river rising to dangerous heights. The town watched helplessly as the water level rose and logs began to create a jam pushing on the pillars of the bridge. When the bridge could no longer hold the weight, the sole access to the other side of town crumbled. The only way to the outside world was now by helicopter. No power, no fresh water, no sewage and no bridge. On February 7, 1990 a new bridge was completed and commemorated in person by Queen Elizabeth II.

Upon arrival, I gave the kids just two weeks of summer break. It was harsh, I know. Now that we lived in the Southern hemisphere the school year was in full swing. We had completed school in Michigan and left no time for summer cavorting before stepping onto the plane.

But what were they supposed to do in the middle of a drizzly winter knowing not a soul? We decided to see what Wairoa had to offer.

The *Wairoa District Museum* was a great introduction to the history of the country. This small museum, smack dab in the middle of town, showed us a perspective of the area with great displays giving an overview of the Maori culture and settlement by Europeans. Ok, so it only took an hour to breeze through this little museum and we only went one time, but it helped us acclimate to the new country we lived in.

The museum about sums it up for tourist attractions in Wairoa. A walk down the main street is pleasant and a stop in *Oslers Bakery* is a must! They are specialists in true New Zealand meat pies with a buttery, flakey crust. Warning: Indulging in too many will be certain to give you a heart attack! The line snakes out the door each day as men wait for these delicious pies. Women's plates tend to be filled with a selection from the rows of mouth-watering slice (bar cookies), delicate tea-cookies and cream puffs that fill the bakery cases.

As time passed and we became acquainted with the town and its people, I found myself sitting down at Oslers with a friend. I would order my favorite: a mochachino adorned with pink and white marshmallows in the shape of a teardrop and a cream puff drizzled in chocolate. These little things made me feel special and like I was becoming a local out for tea with the other mums.

Oslers Bakery & Cafe
116 Marine Parade

Wairoa District Museum
142 Marine Parade

www.nzmuseums.co.nz

Tending to the Fire and Laundry

With naiveté I came to New Zealand thinking it would be very similar to home. Boy was I wrong! I soon learned that despite the fact that it is a first-world, English-speaking country, it is vastly different from the United States and I needed to learn to adapt myself in many ways.

Back home in Michigan I had been a stay-at-home mom of three. I was involved in school activities, took care of my family and enjoyed the occasional "girls day out" with other moms. Now, even the challenges of the smallest daily tasks could push me to the point of tears.

Central heating is as foreign of a concept to a New Zealander as putting beets on a hamburger was to me. My first big challenge was to keep the house warm with a wood-burning stove. But before we could have a fire, we needed to acquire some wood. We found a guy who sold it, rang him up and had it delivered. The kids spent half a day unloading the wood and stacking it in the backyard shed.

With wood on hand, the idea was to build a fire in the morning and keep it burning all day long. The house actually had two wood-burning stoves, one in the family room and another in the kitchen. This was just too much for me to handle. My life simply could not be spent running from stove to stove, throwing wood on all day long. So we made do with only the stove in the family room. We found that by shutting the door to one half of the house we could keep the kitchen and family room bearably warm. Each morning I would lay in bed for a few minutes trying to convince myself to pull back the covers. I would jump with lightning speed out of my jammies and into my clothes, then make a mad dash for the kitchen, which hopefully had some lingering warmth left from the day before. After a bit of hopping up and down and rubbing my hands together I would feel the blood flow—returning me to life.

Chad would typically start the fire for the day, but he had to work, which meant that I had to keep that blasted fire going the rest of the day. I soon learned that tending a fire was much like caring for a baby. I found myself planning my day around when I would have to add more wood to the fire. I could manage one-and-a-half hours to run out to the grocery store, or walk my daughter to school, but if someone asked me to tea I always first thought, "Will I be able to keep the fire going?"

One morning I found myself in a bit of a hurry. It was my first "parent's day" at the primary school and I was very excited to see what my daughter's new life was like. Before I left, I cleaned out the fireplace. I put the ashes in a plastic bucket because there wasn't a metal one in the house. I set it on the floor, got a fire started and forgot about it. I went to the school for a few carefree hours then came home to tend the fire. I noticed an odd smell, looked around and saw the plastic bucket sitting on the floor. In a panic I picked it up and the bottom, which had melted away, fell to the floor. I looked in horror at a pile of red coals on the old wool carpet. I ran and grabbed another bucket—plastic again. Frantically I shoveled the coals into the bucket and ran out to the driveway as I felt the bottom sagging and melting away. Common sense told me that I needed to pour water on the carpet to make sure the fire was not still smoldering. Another voice told me that water would leave a stinky, ashy mess on the floor. In a moment of brilliance I decided to vacuum up the coals. I ran to the closet, grabbed the vacuum cleaner and quickly sucked up what I had missed with the shovel. Reality dawned on me as I looked at the vacuum cleaner with a bag full of age-old dust, now smoldering with hot coals. With shaking hands and tears running down my face, I made another trip as fast as I could out to the driveway to deposit hot coals and melting plastic. I threw water on the floor and called Chad in complete hysterics. He came home quickly, afraid the house was indeed "burning down." Thankfully God saved us from my stupidity. Chad cut the area of burned carpet out to be sure the under-floor was not smoldering. For months we lived with an ugly, gaping hole in the carpet. A clear reminder to me that plastic and hot coals do not mix.

Another amenity I had been accustomed to in the States was a dryer for my clothes. The thought that the entire world did not have a washing machine and a dryer had never entered my mind. Maybe in Africa where the hot sun beats down on the cracked, dry earth, a dryer would not be needed. This was the North Island of New Zealand where it rains a fair amount and is cold and damp three quarters of the year.

Now, I have never really minded doing laundry. In the States I did it once a week and it took me around six hours from putting the first load into the washer to putting the last item folded and ironed into the drawer. I have a ritual: wash and dry everything, then put in a movie to watch while I fold. Lastly I do the ironing. About the time I've completed ironing, the movie is finished and the kids can put their piles away.

But without a dryer, how do I handle that? I remembered seeing a clothes rack in the backyard and lines strung up under the carport. I began to look at the neighborhood with new eyes. Every yard seemed to have laundry flapping in the breeze. What used to be a six hour job turned into a twelve to fifteen hour job. This was partly due to the fact that the washing machine only held half of what my previous machine did. And so a new ritual was born.

On Friday I would check the weather forecast to see what the weekend held. I picked the best looking day and started first thing in the morning. I learned that heavy items such as jeans and towels needed to be in one of the first loads. When the load was completed I took it out to the line and hung it up. It took ten minutes to hang one load of laundry. Things I didn't want to fade from the sun went under the carport, and everything else in the backyard. At first I did not want my underwear hanging out in clear view for the neighborhood to see, so I had a system. I hung bras and panties in the center of the clothes tree and worked my way outward with large and less scandalous items such as t-shirts and towels. The thought of our friends popping by and my bright red bra just hanging there on display horrified me. I relaxed a bit about this when I noticed everyone else's underwear hung in plain sight. No one cared.

After a few hours things began to dry, so I started to bring them in. Air-drying requires a bit more ironing, as things tend to be a bit stiff and crunchy. The last few loads needed to stay out all night because they didn't dry before I went to bed.

The winter proved to be a challenge. Some things took days to dry. The clothes left on the line overnight would be frozen stiff. I had a drying rack I put in front of the fire. All evening I would rotate damp things off the line into the house to dry. I visited friends' homes and they typically had laundry strung-up around their fire as well. It was just part of the decor of a New Zealand home. Things were usually folded and put away still a bit damp. I learned that within the first thirty minutes of wearing something, it would finish drying. Eventually this became a new part of my routine as I found a rhythm to this simpler life.

Gangs

The Global Peace Index measures the personal well being and safety of people by looking at the actions of government, the country's relationship with the world, and the attitudes of its population. New Zealand is at the top of this list, making it the safest country to visit—in the world! So the second thing that put Wairoa on the map must be taken with a grain of salt. Gang violence. There are two main gangs in New Zealand—who knew?—the Mongrel Mob and Black Power.

Every day I walked Elena, my ten-year-old daughter, to school. We left our cozy little cul-de-sac hand in hand, then turned down the alley between two houses. The alley was lined in high, corrugated tin with colorful streaks of graffiti slashed across the silver metal. Bougainvillea vines from the adjoining yard draped over the wall, further decorating the otherwise gloomy corridor. We came out on a main road then continued to the school. It was only a few blocks, but there was one particular house we had to pass, there was no avoiding it. Each morning a known gang member would be hanging around by the driveway, his wild, black, curly hair pulled back with a headband. He always wore red and black. Every morning he smiled and said "hi." We nodded as I unconsciously gripped Elena's hand a bit tighter. It didn't take me long to realize that just because he was in a gang that did not mean that he was a threat to me.

In Wairoa groups of young men walked along the street dressed in black and red, wearing red bandanas. This is thick in the heart of Mongrel Mob country. Driving out of town buildings are tagged by one gang or the other. Clashes occurred. In spite of that, I never felt afraid of jogging around a little knot of gang members because the struggle was not with me. I was just a *pakeha*—a non-Maori person. The struggle was between the black and blue of Black Power and black and red of the Mongrel Mob.

Sometimes I would see a man with a large, round patch sewn to the back of his black leather jacket. A fist or a bulldog popped out from the center. A shiver would crawl up my spine. The red and black threads and lettering spoke of power and intimidation, designed to instill fear. Word was that to receive a patch the wearer had to do something very horrible, like kill another person. So there was a weird tension; these gang members seem to be very lonely people looking for something to fill the void. They do horrible things and turn to violence, drugs and alcohol to find acceptance with other lost souls. But they are very little threat to anyone outside the gang world.

Regardless, I never felt comfortable enough to let my daughter walk alone to school.

Once Were Warriors – A movie about the gangs in New Zealand.

School

We left Michigan just as school was ending in June and arrived in Wairoa in the middle of their school year. Moving to the southern hemisphere created its own set of problems. Do we hold the kids back and have them repeat half a school year only to be behind when we return home or jump ahead half a year and hope they survive? We decided to risk the jump and do a bit of extra work at home. It didn't take long to realize that the "little bit of extra work at home" would be to keep the kids up to American standards rather than trying to catch up in their new classrooms.

Even though the equivalent grade in New Zealand was behind that of the United States in areas like math and English, I soon saw how my kids' education had broadened. I had never studied World War II from any country's perspective except my own. To learn how such a tiny nation was deeply influenced and affected by sending her sons off to die in the same battles our ancestors perished in greatly moved me.

We kept up with English by family participation in a blog, science sorted itself out, and history and humanities were improved by the move, so only math remained deficient.

I know I am not cut out to be a homeschool mom. I don't want my kids to graduate from school and struggle their entire lives because I tried to teach them myself. It's just not in me. It's not who I am. It's good to know your strengths and weaknesses and to be honest with yourself about them. So I contacted a few friends who are amazing homeschool moms, checked out a few resources and decided on a math curriculum that the kids could pretty much teach themselves. They didn't particularly like it, but handled the additional work with grace. Each day after school they sat down at the table and did one additional math lesson. It paid off—when we returned home they were ahead of their class!

Public school in a foreign country was an amazing experience. It's where we made friends, learned about the culture, tried new sports and found opportunities to explore the country.

School uniforms were a new concept to us. As a mom I am all for them. There was less laundry to do and less time figuring out what to wear. Elena, who was in elementary school, had a comfy sweatsuit and a hat to block the sun while Maddie and Damon, in middle and high school, had pants, polo shirts and sweatshirts. It wasn't overly hoity-toity but everybody wore the same thing.

The school campuses were designed different than the large buildings with endless hallways that I was accustomed to back home. The Mediterranean climate didn't require architects to work as hard to keep out frigid temperatures. Sun was in abundance and the style of buildings allowed kids to enjoy the outdoors even when walking between classrooms. Hallways were outdoors with awnings and led to courtyards filled with flowers and playground equipment.

Just another thing that made me feel welcome and relaxed in New Zealand.

Saxon homeschool products
http://saxonhomeschool.hmhco.com/en/saxonhomeschool.htm

<u>Small Town Fun</u>

How does one entertain oneself without a movie theater, no large bookstore to peruse or mall to wander? Time keeps a different pace in New Zealand, much more relaxed and laid-back. But for a city girl all the familiar ways of entertaining myself were gone.

For as long as I can remember I have wanted to learn how to dance. I have memories of Saturday evenings with my sister prancing around the family room in long flannel nightgowns and pink curlers while Lawrence Welk, with conductor's baton in hand, took Norma Zimmer, in her floor-length chiffon dress, and floated across the dance floor. My dreams matured to *Dancing with the Stars* as my neighbor and I "knowledgeably" critiqued the stars from the couch while munching on popcorn.

My dreams came true when we moved to Wairoa and my husband surprised me by taking me to dance lessons. It was the social thing to do in our little town. The graceful and the clumsy gathered together in the school gym to practice and learn new steps.

Our teacher, Lynda, was the middle-aged daughter of the local sawmill owner. Dancing was her passion. She worked at the mill during the day, but at night she opened up the school gymnasium and offered ballroom dance lessons. Her vibrancy and flair attracted townsfolk from all backgrounds. Farmers drove in from secluded homes, bankers and doctors walked from a few blocks over and teachers just hung out after school was finished. We all came together to dance.

Dancing is not as easy as it looks. The first few weeks were very frustrating for Chad and I as we struggled with how to manage four left feet. We didn't know what direction to go or who was really leading. Those first weeks most of our energy seemed to go into avoiding knocking or being knocked over, stepping on one another's toes and mid-dance marital therapy. Slowly we began to feel more comfortable with moving our feet to different rhythms. I started to relax enough to recognize when my husband was trying to move me in a certain direction, and over time I began to feel the music.

Eventually we had our first dance. The theme was "The Wild West." The day of the dance I was walking downtown with a friend and we ran into another girl from our class. We excitedly exchanged notes on what we were going to wear and what we were bringing to eat. You would have thought we were a couple of schoolgirls getting ready for prom!

That evening we arrived at the dance hall, put our food down and found some seats. We began visiting. Getting out there and dancing was something neither of us was feeling overly courageous to attempt. I watched my friends foxtrot across the floor, swirling and twirling led by their partners. We were saved by other people who had been at it for several years asking us to dance. The men were quite comfortable with just pushing me around the floor. My feet tangled and we would pause. I pulled myself together over and over again until I began to understand my role as the woman in a dance. The evening was social as we began chatting with the people in our class.

Norm, an elderly friend from class, asked me to dance. As I gained confidence in my moves, he began to reminisce. He shared stories of dancing with his late wife. His eyes grew distant as he remembered those nights in the 40's, swinging her around. During the war it was quite the rage in Wairoa to dance until dawn at one of the seven different halls. I stumbled a bit and his eyes refocused. I felt honored to have a momentary glimpse through the window to his heart.

Learning to dance with my husband taught me a lot about myself. I wanted to lead. I wanted the dance to go my way. I was positive that I knew what I was doing and would take control. Often we would go in two different directions only to bump into each other. This would result in a cold stare, a harsh word and frustration. I began to learn that when I focused on the gentle push to my hand to move me in a certain direction, the dance would go smoothly. Sometimes I just need to stop and listen to the gentle push moving me along in life.

The Garden

One of the first things I noticed about our backyard was a nice plot of ground tucked in the corner. The dark, black, fertile soil that had once been someone's garden beckoned to me to produce life in it once again. My horticultural experience up to this point in life was a little bruschetta garden of tomatoes and basil along-side the house. We'd never had a yard large enough to have a full garden, so now I began to dream of all the fresh produce that I would have at my fingertips.

I really had no idea where to begin so I got out my "Square Foot Gardening" book that a friend had sent with me. She has gorgeous gardens with raised wooden boxes to keep the critters out. Trellises hold melon plants heavy with fruit. She talks of picking, freezing, canning and, best of all, eating fruits and vegetables she's grown. Words like "aerating" and "blanching" were not even in my vocabulary, but I wanted them to be. So I poured over the book underlining, marking pages and drawing up a plan. I was going to grow a garden!

One day as I wandered the yard, checking on the progress of the fruit trees and dreaming of this bountiful garden that I would soon have, I noticed my neighbor in his backyard.

I had already met Stew over the fence a few times. He was a man who seemed younger than his seventy-two years. He had a bounce to his step and a gleam in his eye. He reminded me of Wilson from Home Improvement. With a fisherman's hat perched on his balding head, his eyes sparkled over the wooden fence to greet me. He always had a wise word and a bit of encouragement to share. Stew's backyard overflowed with colorful flowers and fruit trees ready to be picked. If I thought my backyard was the Garden of Eden, then his backyard was Heaven itself.

I called Stew over to the fence.

"Could you give me some advice on planting a garden?" I asked.

"Well sure, Kris. First you're going to need to turn over that dirt. Then you need to buy some plants and get them in the ground. How about if I take you and my wife, Val, over to The Greenhouse to pick out your plants and have a smoko."

Although I was completely confused as to what the plan was, I figured I could execute step one: turn over the soil.

The next day there was a rapping on the door. I found Stew standing there with his hat on his head, gumboots on his feet (otherwise known as black rubber boots), and a shovel in his hand.

"I've come to turn over your garden for you Kris."

My jaw dropped open. Stew was seventy-two years old! Even though I was in the middle of kneading some bread, I dashed out the screen door after him, with my apron still tied around my waist. I grabbed my gumboots and a shovel that I had seen in the shed.

"Oh no Kris, I'm going to turn this dirt over for you. You head back into the house and I'll pick you up tomorrow at 11:00 to buy some plants and have a smoko." My shoulders dropped a bit as I returned to my bread.

At 11:00 the next day I was ready. I was going plant shopping! I had my list in hand as we walked through the greenhouse. I breathed in the scent of flowers mingled with fresh, moist soil as I picked out what would go in my garden. Green beans, carrots, zucchini, melon, tomatoes, swiss chard... I carried my precious little bundles up to the cash register and paid for them. Then I joined Stew and Val at a table in the coffee shop.

I learned that although he had a "cuppa," Stew did not go out for "tea." I was still baffled by the "smoko" part of the outing. I asked. Stew talked about the days when he worked in the factory. He would join his friends for a mid-day break to smoke a cigarette. He gave up smoking years ago but the term stuck. Now any sort of informal break in his day—even tea with his wife—was called a smoko.

I was jumping with excitement the next morning at the thought of getting my little plants into the freshly turned dirt. A knock at the door once again startled me into action. There was Stew in his gumboots carrying a basket of string, a tape measure, small garden tools and other miscellaneous items.

"I've come to plant your garden for you, Kris." he announced.

I felt a little disappointment seep into my soul. I got my boots and headed out with him. Full of animation I showed him how I wanted to do the garden in squares. What plants would go in which square and how they could grow in harmony. My friend's book had helped me plan everything.

"No, no." he scoffed. "We'll plant rows because that's how gardens are made."

And with a wave of his hand, it was settled.

In hindsight, rows were best for this garden. My squares would have looked ridiculous and it would have been a disaster trying to weed a three-foot by three-foot grid in the thick, black soil. People said, "You drop a nail and a week later there's a crowbar growing in the spot." I couldn't wait to see what would come of my little seedlings!

During those first few days in the garden with Stew I planted more than just a few frail seedlings. What we really planted that day was a friendship that would develop over the fence. A moment here, a few words there. "How's the garden growing?" "How did your cricket team do last night?" Visits to Stew and Val's house for tea and even a Tupperware party became frequent additions to my normal routine.

Square Foot Gardening: A New Way to Garden in Less Space with Less Work
By: Mel Bartholomew
Publisher: Rodale Press, Inc.

Food

"Comfort food is prepared in a traditional style having a usually nostalgic or sentimental appeal."[2] For me food is a tie to home. It brings me a warm feeling from the inside out on a rainy day. Family conversation would turn to remembering food when we were homesick or the days had just become too long. Sometimes when I was longing for home I could almost taste my old favorites. Going out to dinner often turned into a disappointing experience when the entrees presented just didn't do anything for my taste buds. Now don't get me wrong. I enjoy trying new foods when I am visiting a new place, but living in a foreign country I found that I began to long for ingredients and foods that I could only find at home.

We quickly learned that New Zealand is not known for its cuisine. It does not have the divine pastries of France, the spicy food of Mexico or the rich pastas and sauces of Italy. It is a British colony and so it's not surprising that their food is bland and tasteless.

Even falling back on the old faithful "hamburger and fries" became a study in disappointment. Nothing beats a big, juicy cheddar cheeseburger with tomato, lettuce and ketchup. Mouth watering, I tried ordering this a few times only to have my hopes dashed into the ground as I was served some form of meatloaf burger with beets and an egg piled on top. And what about ordering pizza in, only to have barbeque sauce squirted all over the top? I would nibble away at the food as my appetite ran out the back door.

Forget a good-old-fashioned American hot dog. In New Zealand, no gathering was complete without a "sausage sizzle." Whether a school function, sports team party, family gathering or fundraiser, sausages would be the main attraction. It was the equivalent to pizza at American gatherings. There was a distinct science to the "sausage sizzle." The only type of sausage available was a low cost, pureed meat sausage with very little flavor added. It was cooked on a propane "grill" that consisted of a flat iron surface that amounts to a frying pan. The sausage was wrapped in a piece of heavily buttered cheap white bread, slathered in tomato sauce and stuck in a serviette (napkin) before being handed to you. After being there a year I had buttered more slices of bread than I could count and turned as many sausages on the grill. I was amazed at the number of sausages that were consumed each time. I was not sad to say "goodbye" to sausages when we left New Zealand, but the process of making and eating sausages in a group of people pulled me closer to the community.

Every once in awhile I would see something staring at me from the pastry case at Oslers that I couldn't resist trying. Lollie Cake was one such temptation. A plate held slices of cake made with colorful candies, covered in a glass dome. This cake looked happy and inviting. Lollie Cake is made of crushed malt cookies, corn syrup, condensed milk and Eskimo lollies, better known as Circus Peanuts. Ah, why had I never thought of such a concoction? Cake with Circus Peanuts! I tenderly carried my slice over to the table. I took a bite, smiling at the sugary sweetness. One bite was all that I could handle. I could feel the sugar hit my veins as I sat there trying not to bounce on my chair!

Going to the grocery store was always a new adventure. There were boxes filled with foods I was not familiar with. For a country with some of the best dairy in the world, it was perplexing to have boxed milk on the shelf. I never got used to the mental concept of shelf-stable milk and went a full year without drinking a glass. I couldn't have done that if Oreos were available, but they weren't.

I was stumped at the poor selection of cereals as I browsed in the grocery store. In Meijers back home, an entire, endless aisle was devoted to cereal. Colorful boxes with cartoon animals peeking out at me made selecting a flavor fun. I began to ask my friends what they ate for breakfast.

"Toast with Marmite. Here, try some."

And with that I found myself staring at a piece of toast spread with a thin layer of brown goo. I gulped, took a deep breath and slowly bit into the toast. My mouth erupted in disgust while my face struggled to keep from revealing my horror. Putting the toast down while gagging on my words I asked, "What in the world is that stuff?"

Marmite, first produced in Britain, is a concentrated form of brewer's yeast. Following the adage "waste not, want not," Marmite uses the leftover sludge from the beer brewing process. Of course they add vitamins and vegetables to try to dress it up a bit, but really it's just yeast sludge. Yuck. The term likely is derived from the small ceramic jars it was sold in that resembled the French casserole dish called a "marmite." New Zealand produces its own Marmite which has a very distinct flavor. Even your typical Marmite consumer is fussy about which variety they eat. I have never met an American who has a fondness for this product. You either love it or you hate it. Marmite can stay in the back of the cupboard when I'm visiting.

I looked at people oddly when they asked me if I wanted some "fush and chups" for dinner. What? Oh, "fish and chips!" I'm always on the hunt for a good platter of fish and chips. With just the right amount of batter, a bit of salt, and a little grease soaking the paper it's wrapped in, the fish melts in your mouth.

In New Zealand, fish and chips is the equivalent to take-out pizza in America. I discovered the local fish and chips shop, Ponderosa, on the other side of the river in the more or less abandoned part of town. Despite the location, there was always a line out the door with a few people mingling outside. There was plenty to choose from beyond the standard breaded and fried fish. If it's seafood and you want it fried, they had it. We would call ahead on Saturday night and give our order of "eight fish and two scoops (of french fries) please." Fifteen minutes later I walked out with two bundles of steaming food. At home I laid it on the counter, we opened the greasy layers of newspaper it was wrapped in, got out the Heinz (no New Zealand tomato sauce was going to spoil those chips!) and dug in. This fish just literally melted in your mouth. A five-star restaurant could not have done better. I savored every bite.

One night we decided to really splurge and get dessert as well—a fried Moro bar. A Moro bar is Cadbury's equivalent to a Milky Way. Now whoever thought of battering and frying a candy bar was a bit out of their mind. The first bite melted in my mouth and I thought I was in heaven. The second bite was disgusting and by the third bite I felt like I was in the pit of hell.

Now that I am no longer in New Zealand, I long for a plate of fish and chips from Ponderosa. I look at a menu and wonder if the fish will live up to my expectations. The waiter will tell me "Our fish and chips are excellent." I order them and am always disappointed.

There are days when the only thing that will get you through is a taste of home. To say that I love McDonald's is an understatement. A double cheeseburger, french fries and coke does more than just fill me up. It is the pure essence of comfort food. It makes me feel warm, happy, relaxed. It evokes memories of high school away games, traveling on the bus and stopping for dinner. High on post-game excitement, french fries were alternately devoured and thrown at the back of friends' heads. Then as a young mom, I met friends at McDonald's while we let the kids loose in the play area. Talking for hours, we would sip a cheap cup of cappuccino, the conversation flowing. Fortunately the kids made it through that time of life without a case of hand, foot, and mouth disease!

In recent years, McDonald's brings memories of traveling with the kids and my sister to visit my parents. Parked beneath the Golden Arches, we would pile out of the van with a hoard of children in tow. Mainly we stopped because my sister knew it was my favorite restaurant and she took pity on me! The cousins would all cram into a booth together while my sister and I sat at a different table—peace for a few minutes before we all loaded back into the van.

I actually only eat at McDonald's once a month because I know that more often will be a slow death to my body. My last meal at McDonald's before we left for New Zealand was with intention. I planned the day I would need a quick meal and I looked forward to it for two weeks. Because I was short on time I decided to use the drive-through. I pulled up to the speaker stand and said, "double cheeseburger value meal with ketchup only." I paid and pulled away with my cheap food in a paper bag. I was truly in heaven anticipating this last meal. I pulled onto the road, opened my sandwich and took a bite. They had totally messed up my order. The sandwich had everything but ketchup! I didn't have time to go back and correct the order. I wanted to cry as I ate my messed up burger. My final meal at McDonald's was so disappointing.

Yes, they do have McDonald's in New Zealand, but the closest one to our town was an hour-and-a-half away. Seven weeks with no McDonald's—my blood was running thin. I took the kids to Napier for a day extravaganza. I packed sack lunches for a carefree picnic on the beach. We went to the aquarium and did some errands around town. By late afternoon the kids were complaining that they were hungry. I had no resolve left. We were going to McDonald's. I pulled in and began to feel my toes twinkle; energy ran through me. We opened the doors and the heavens sang—Ahh, Ahh, Ahh! My jaw dropped to the ground. It was huge! I was like a kid in a candy shop. To the left was "McCafe." It had a glass case with tortes and cheesecakes—and a real cappuccino machine, its stainless steal glistening. Ahead of me was the restaurant. They did have some funky sandwiches—no Big Mac, but rather, a Kiwi Burger. Who wants *beetroot* on their burger?? I searched the menu and YES, they had a double cheeseburger! We placed our order and sat down. I opened my sandwich, breathing in the greasy scent. I took a bite. After seven weeks of onions in hamburger patties, I had finally found some American food. Everything seemed right with the world as we ate our dinner—or as they said on that side of the world, tea.

In New Zealand there were many meanings to the word "tea." Damon went to squash practice one afternoon with a friend from school. The mother rang me and asked if I would mind if she picked up some fish and chips for Damon's tea. In a bit of confusion I said this would be fine. Listening closer as people talked, I found that "supper" was referred to as "tea."

Another reference to tea was "morning tea." I had several invitations to morning tea. Much to my surprise, it was a somewhat formal affair. I had been assured that Kiwis were very informal and relaxed with their tea, yet each time it was a treat for me. There was an etiquette to the affair. Cups and saucers were matched with place mats and napkins. Sugar and cream were set out with the tea. Delightful finger foods were served little sandwiches, breads, crackers with hot sauce and cheese, and biscuits (cookies). A little sweet and a little savory. Conversation during tea was polite and cheerful. One had to be adept at small talk.

Another form of tea was when one just popped over to a friend or neighbor's house during the day and you were offered a cup of tea. This was a very relaxed time. Put as much sugar in your tea as you like and conversation went to the heart of the matter; no pretenses there. I decided to give this a try one day when a neighbor stopped in. I offered her a cup of tea and some cookies that I had made. "God, you're domestic." was her comment. I found her to be a rather colorful woman as we continued in conversation. No pretenses there!

Lollie Cake
By Kristen Faber

½ cup butter, melted
1 cup sweetened condensed milk
1 cup malt biscuits, crushed (gram crackers are the best American substitute)
7 ounces circus peanuts, chopped
Sweetened coconut, shaved

1. Stir together melted butter and sweetened condensed milk and allow to cool.
2. Mix in malt biscuits and circus peanuts.
3. Shape into a log then roll in the coconut to coat.
4. Place in fridge until firm. Cut into slices.

Ponderosa Fish Shop
32 Carroll St.
North Clyde, Wairoa

The Maori

Around 1250, several waves of settlers arrived in New Zealand by waka (a Maori boat) from Eastern Polynesia. They were isolated from the rest of the world and began to develop a separate culture with a language, performing arts, decorative crafts and a rich mythology. This unique culture became known as the "Maori." The word "Maori" originally meant "the local people." Upon the arrival of white Europeans it took on the meaning of "the original people" as opposed to the "pakeha," a term the Maori created when they first heard the unfamiliar sounds that Captain Cook's crew made.

The Maori settled mainly on the east coast, preferring the temperate climate. Despite being a stone age culture with no knowledge of metal, they were very advanced in their technology using bone from birds, dogs, whales and even humans, as well as stone to create tools and weapons. Tribal groups formed as settlement spread. New plants were introduced and horticulture flourished in the rich volcanic soil.

In time, a prominent warrior culture emerged. As tribes spread and further isolated themselves, the need for new gene pools increased. Tribes would travel great distances by foot to club and spear the men of other tribes and take the women as wives and forced slaves. Ferocious in their warfare, they used psychology and intimidation such as the "haka" or war dance. To capture the "mana" or status and respect of the enemy, cannibalism became common and acceptable. Several explorers were eaten, including Marion Du Fresne in 1772 along with sixteen of his crew. This provided a needed source of protein in the Maori diet until the arrival of the Europeans who introduced pigs and cattle.

In an account from Captain Cook, he records:

"There was not a man aboard Endeavour who, in the event of the ship's breaking up, would not have preferred to drown rather than be left to the mercy of the Maoris. For as Endeavour slowly circled the North Island, those few words spoken by the Maori boys—'Do not put us ashore there; it is inhabited by our enemies who will kill and eat us'—began to grow into a hideous reality. Yet even as fresh evidence came to light that these people were indeed cannibals, the ship's company still refused to believe the truth their eyes told them.

Tupia inquired if it was their practice to eat men, to which they answered in the affirmative; but said that they ate only their enemies who were slain in battle. We now began seriously to believe that this horrid custom prevailed amongst them, for what the boys had said we had considered as a mere hyperbolical expression of their fear. But some days later some of our people found in the skirts of the wood, near a hole, or oven, three human hip-bones, which they brought on board: a further proof that these people eat human flesh..."[3]

Overall, the Maori lived a good life until the European settlers came in the late eighteenth century. Small skirmishes occurred, but fortunately England seemed to have learned a thing or two from settling America and introduced the "Treaty of Waitangi." On February 6, 1840 the British Crown and approximately five-hundred-forty Maori chiefs signed this agreement. The political contract between the two countries aimed to establish a government in New Zealand. The treaty recognized the Maori as the original inhabitants of the land, gave British protection to the Maori, and promised land and fishing rights. Differences in the signed English and Maori versions have caused debate that continues today.

Gradually the Maori adopted much of the Western culture. Today the Maori make up fifteen percent of New Zealand's population with ninety percent living on the North Island.

Films such as *Whale Rider* do an excellent job of depicting life in a Maori community. I found many of the social dynamics portrayed to be consistent with my experience in a small, mainly Maori town. Single parent homes, abuse, alcoholism and gangs are struggles the people face continually. Mysticism is a strong element evident even in life today.

In the 1960's a movement to protect their culture arose. A resurgence of mokos (tattooing), especially done in the traditional manner, is occurring. The Maori take this sign of cultural identity very seriously and feel that the bearer must earn the right to display a facial moko. Men especially are proud to wear tattoos on their buttocks, thighs, backs and stomachs. Ancestral and tribal messages specific to the wearer are woven into the designs indicating "value" through genealogy and social status. Instead of using a needle to insert dye, the Maori carved into the skin with chisels, leaving grooves in the skin rather than natural smoothness. Soot and fat were combined to make the pigment, which was rubbed into the raw grooves. It takes a very skilled artist to create this type of moko. It is easy to distinguish a traditional moko over a modern moko. Traditional tattoo lines are darker in color and a thin, precise scar rises on the skin. The moko may seem scary or odd the first time you see one, but over time a beauty appears through the pattern. Pride and confidence of Maori identity is noticed in the person. Of particular intrigue to me were the facial tattoos. I think this is because one would need to have very strong reasons to alter their face with tattoos and I admired the strength of identity I saw in those who wore the moko. We all look at the faces of people who pass by us. Small details of a stranger's face will come to mind later. We identify people through these features, so when a man's face is fully tattooed with intricate patterns or a woman's lips are dyed black and her chin covered in a Maori pattern, we recognize a pride of association.

The kapa haka encompasses the cultural dances of the Maori. A visit to Rotorua provides a nice opportunity to eat a traditional hungi (meal) and view a kapa haka with an explanation of its history. But my favorite time to see the kapa haka was in the schools. My eight-year-old daughter, Elena, jumped right in, barely understanding the New Zealand accent let alone the Maori songs of the kapa haka.

On performance day we rode the bus to a neighboring town where many primary schools had gathered to celebrate the kapa haka. The kids changed into their pupus (grass skirts) and woven tops. Chin mokos were applied with makeup. Grass hairpieces that they had woven in class adorned their heads. Giggles and songs floated around the room— excitement was in the air. We found places on the grass in front of the outdoor stage. Perched on a cliff overlooking the ocean, the waves danced in the wind as children from area schools danced on stage. Their songs and chants rose above the voice of the sea crashing against the cliffs.

Soon my daughter was on stage surrounded by her new friends. I heard a man and a woman on stage chanting back and forth. The children waited for their cue. The large Maori man moved his arms in great gestures while the woman moved her hands up and down in a trembling motion known as wiri. I noticed that many dances included the wiri which signifies an interface between the body and mind. A young girl responded in a melodic chant and the boys answered by taking their spears and stomping in a warrior like pose. Thus began their performance of simple melodies, rhythmic chants and choreographed dances. Elena swung her hips while her grass skirt swayed and her poi (two balls attached to a cord) swung in circles in unison with the other girls. Hitting the poi to change the direction of the twirl created another rhythm. A stomp of the foot and sway of the hips indicated the transition between songs and more chanting. Concluding their performance the girls stepped back as the boys stomped forward. With ferociousness beyond their eight years, they squatted like tiny warriors and stomped in rhythm. Their faces contorted into scary scowls as every muscle in their bodies began to shiver with intensity. The haka—the warrior challenge—was about to begin. The boys loved performing the haka at every opportunity. Often a haka would break out spontaneously among a small group of boys at school assemblies. Other boys would join in as the girls, teachers and parents would cheer and applaud. Their energy level was high that morning, the challenge in their eyes begging an opponent. The stage shook as they pounded the ground with their feet. The clawing at their chests drew blood, but they didn't notice. These miniature men did a performance worthy of the national rugby team, the All Blacks. They ended with their faces terrifyingly contorted and tongues hanging out. Youtube is filled with videos of the haka. A great example to watch is the All Blacks in their pre-game ritual.

Elena walked off the stage with a smile filling her face. I was so proud of my little girl who had jumped in wholeheartedly to join in this cultural celebration. Watching the older kids, I noticed the intensity had grown. They had mastered the pukana or "glaring" of the eyes in which their lips were pulled back to reveal teeth and their eyes bugged out. With a slight tip of the head they could turn the terror on and off like the flip of a switch.

The Marae

I quickly found that "stay-at-home mums" are a rare commodity in New Zealand. The cost of living is high and it is simply a necessity to work. So I found my daytime social group to be mainly elderly people. It didn't bother me in the least. There were lots of stories to be heard and wisdom to be imparted. There were other benefits as well. I volunteered to help with a Senior Citizen health and wellness group. Eventually I had the privildge of being invited into the local marae (meeting house).

There are thirty-three marae in the Wairoa area. The Maori attend a marae based on family history rather than geography. We drove a little out of town before coming to the marae. People were arriving and greeting one another with a hongi. The hongi is the traditional Maori greeting; men touch their foreheads and noses together in an intimate yet warm gesture, whereas the women touch cheeks and kiss. This is only done on one side, unlike the French who kiss on each cheek. With the old women the kisses tended to be familiar and wet. It was only proper to kiss every person, which took a bit of time and a few tissues.

As we milled around kissing one another, a man suddenly called out in Maori song from inside the fence. A woman outside the gate answered with another song. They sang a short banter back and forth before we were invited into the marae.

We entered under a carved arch painted in red and white. In the center of the arch was another carving—a mask representing the original chief of the marae. Carvings on either side of the entrance represented different families of importance. History was woven into their most important community structure. Entering, we sat on benches along the outside fence. As a sign of stature and societal place, the men sat on the front bench with the women seated behind.

The formal part of the ceremony began with a welcome and a song before the Catholic priest from Wairoa spoke. Another song commenced and then a man got up and spoke. He gave the recent birth, death and wedding announcements as well as other local news. A living newspaper of sorts. The forty-five minute ceremony took place in the Maori language but fortunately I have learned the art of looking clued in when I really have no idea what is happening.

I particularly enjoyed the singing. Some songs were sung only by the five men and women in front and other songs by everyone. A beautiful blending of acappella voices filled the courtyard. There was joy in the sound and festivity in the air. The folk songs recounted the history of the Maori people.

After the welcome, announcements, message and singing, we were invited into the meeting hall. We endured another reception line of leaders while greeting each with another hongi.

The meeting hall had a second more elaborately carved entrance. The marae we were in was very unique because it was a Christian marae. The Catholic church started and runs this particular marae. The carvings tell the story of its beginning. The eagle at the top is the New Zealand Eagle (now extinct) with its wings spread over the entrance representing God. Gold paint throughout also gives reference to God. Carved into the right support are a Catholic Priest and Nun who came to evangelize New Zealand and on the left are traditional Maori figures with Christian references. The rib carvings on the ceiling are representative of the ribs of a whale. The minute detail and symbolism made me realize how little my culture thinks of the structure and design of a space. The Maori pour their history and beliefs into their space, so they are continually reminded of where they came from and who they are.

Tables were laden with food to eat. Scones lathered in butter, grilled cheese and onion sandwiches, split pea and pumpkin soups, cookies and tea to drink. Somehow this diet didn't seem to par with the "wellness" emphasis of the event.

Of course being a senior citizen's meeting, blood pressure was taken, a health talk given, and we had a session of stretching. Conversation was lively, wandering to various topics including a myriad of ailments and the electric scooter several women were thinking about buying to help with getting around! We did an interesting small group exercise brainstorming on how to save energy and save on groceries due to rising costs. As women suggested things like "cook a meal on the wood burning stove" or "use a hot water bottle in bed instead of using the electric blanket" or "grow, shoot and home make your food," I was thinking "All I want to do is keep the fire going for one whole day so I can stay warm!"

I became a regular attender at these monthly meetings. The women adopted me as one of their own even though they were thirty years my senior and of a different race and culture. I became comfortable playing cards with them while discussing their aches and pains. A sense of community grew between us as we shared our lives with each other.

Mahia

One of my favorite day get-aways was the little beach town of Mahia only thirty minutes from our house. New Zealand is speckled with these tiny towns. There is nothing touristy about them. Little communities with a town bar that serves mouth-watering fish n' chips. A bay with a local beach where people hangout for the day breathing in the fresh salty air. Fishing competitions where massive creatures are pulled from the sea. It is where New Zealand becomes home and the tales of the ocean come true.

Things in small towns are never done quite the way city culture would find appropriate. For example, my uncle had a boat when I was a kid. He would pull the boat out to Lake Michigan with his car to spend a day on the water. Backing the boat into the marina, everyone waved their arms and shouted conflicting directions. Then we would walk onto the dock and hop into the boat to be off for a day of jumping the waves.

One winter day I sat on the beach in Mahia killing a bit of time and giving the kids a chance to run around. Snuggled deep into a blanket, I had the rest of the beach to myself. It was much too cold to swim but we needed little excuse to be on the beach. Across the water I noticed a small fishing boat come into the bay and pull up to the shore. The next thing I knew, a guy jumped out of the boat into chest-deep water and waded to shore. He climbed onto a large, old, red farming tractor which had a boat trailer attached to it. He backed into the water, the boat drove up onto the trailer and the tractor drove off down the street. I looked around and suddenly it hit me that the parking lot was full of tractors, all with boat trailers attached to them. A little while later another boat came into the bay and the same thing happened. The man jumped out of the boat and a few minutes later he was put-putting toward home, boat in tow.

As I left town my eyes were opened to something new. Many houses had tractors parked in their front yards. For some reason I found this completely hysterical. How would it look in my nice little suburban neighborhood back home for every other house to have a boat in the drive and a tractor in the yard? These little things made life colorful and kept us smiling.

<u>A New Friend</u>

From the moment we stepped foot in Wairoa we heard stories of a Bottlenose dolphin who was reported to swim with the locals. Ok, I know it's New Zealand where everything wild is possible, but really? We were anxious to meet this dolphin and jumped at the chance when our friends, Ruth and Russell, invited us to go kayaking in Mahia with the hopes of meeting Moko.

With kayaks loaded onto their trailer, we headed off to the bay in Mahia for a late afternoon of playing in the cool spring sea. With Ruth and Russell on one kayak, Chad and I got on the other and paddled out into the bay. Mahia is located at the northern tip of Hawke's Bay. The hilly Mahia Peninsula juts south into the sea creating a very sheltered area at Mahia Beach.

Paddling out into the water, I was surrounded by raw cliffs, wooded hills and grassy bluffs. It took my breath away. The calm of the protected bay made paddling easy. Side by side our two kayaks headed further from shore as we each silently took in the beauty. There was no need for words. Each of us was lost in our own thoughts. So small and alone on the ocean, rocking gently. Unexpectedly out of nowhere Moko appeared right next to us flipping his tail as if to say, "You're not alone, I have been following you this whole time!"

I was delighted. Moko swam alongside us, surfacing then disappearing into the deep. Intently, I watched the water looking for his fin to break the surface. Suddenly he would appear, taunting us by staying just out of reach. Under the boat, in front of the boat, then finally next to us where I could tentatively reach out my hand and touch him with my fingers. He didn't seem to mind as he swam steadily next to me, grazing the surface of the water. We laughed, and I squealed. The experience was as much about the joy of interacting with Moko as it was about sharing this encounter with our friends.

Excited to have the kids experience this marvel, we began to paddle into shore. Moko stayed close, teasing us with splashes, guiding the way. The mist from his blowhole sprayed our faces. With Ruth and Russell in the lead we raced with Moko toward the shore. About fifty yards from the beach Moko decided he wasn't done playing with us yet. He came close, I could touch his silky skin. Bottlenoses are large dolphins. They can grow up to fourteen feet long and weigh one thousand one hundred pounds. He laid his seven-foot body next to our kayak and slowly turned us around. We were trapped. I would like to say that I handled this setback with ease, but I didn't. I pretty much flipped out. The harder we paddled to turn ourselves around the more his tail calmly swished in the water.

When in complete panic, I typically lose all ability for rational thinking. My mind stirred up pictures of falling into the water and being eaten by a dolphin. Images of my now parentless children flashed through my mind. Fortunately Russell had made a quick exchange and paddled out to us with their daughter, Suzelle. Moko was easily distracted and swam off to play with the other boat. We headed in and I traded places with one of the kids.

Sinking onto the sandy beach I realized the power of this amazing wild animal we were frolicking with. He was powerful enough to defend an area from sharks yet chose to be gentle while playing with us in the sea. Rubbing my hand along Moko's body, I got a feeling for the strength within him.

As each child floated on the ocean, Moko approached. The joy in discovery was contagious. Together we shared the moments bonding with each other in the sort of way you only can when experiencing a unique gift. The sun was beginning to slip below the horizon. The sky lit up in beautiful shades of yellows, reds, oranges and pinks. The kayakers became silhouettes against the sky with the fin following persistently behind.

After dragging the kayaks to shore the kids ran back into the water. Moko became intimate, laying next to them and allowing the kids to throw their arms around him and take a ride. Elena rode along the shore holding onto his fin. Her hair danced in the breeze. She was oblivious to the world around her. Saying a mournful "goodbye," we wrapped up in sweatshirts and blankets, curled-up in the grass and feasted on fresh, steaming fish n' chips. These moments bonded us forever with our friends.

This was only the beginning of our relationship with Moko. We returned to Mahia Beach time and time again. Most of the time Moko would appear. We brought balls and boogie boards to play with. We grew accustomed to his great form gilding past us. I would lay my hands in the water and he would slide under them as if he wanted to be scratched. His smooth skin felt like rubber. Without hesitation he would swim between my legs, lifting me off the ground in a playful move. He always looked like he was smiling at us, begging us to stay longer. We introduced our friends to him and he always put on a good show.

In the recesses of our minds we knew we had experienced something unique and rare with Moko. Shortly after we left New Zealand, Moko made his way north, stopping in different communities for a bit of time to satisfy his love of people. Not long after, he was found dead on an island beach. Moko made himself famous by rescuing two pygmy sperm whales trapped on a sandbar in Mahia when he was young. Mahia was his home for several years where he became part of the local community. He will forever be remembered in my heart as the gentle creature who lovingly played with us, Once Upon a Time.

Little Delights for Little People

On the other side of Mahia peninsula we would find a place to park along Mahia East Coast Rd. No longer a part of Hawke's Bay, this side of Mahia is open to the wilds of the South Pacific Ocean. Coral flats stretch from the sandy beach into the sea, flooding with the movement of the tide, providing life for all sorts of creatures. Clad in water shoes we would

44

wander these flats for hours searching for treasures. The kids would reach down in delight to pull small shells and tiny crabs from the tidal pools. Waves tumbled over the rocks, curling foaming fingers around our ankles, attempting to pull us down. I would often stand there lost in the movement of the water and air as surfers twisted and turned trying to take advantage of riding each wave that rolled past.

My attention was torn away with a squeal of delight from the kids as they huddled around a small pool of water, their noses only an inch above the surface. Damon carefully reached in and gently pulled a bright orange starfish out of the water. It wriggled and twisted its star points around Damon's fingers. Soft ohs and ahhs were lost in the sound of the waves, but my mother's ears were tuned in to every inflection from my children. They explored the intricacies in the design of this amazing creature as they gently passed it around. With tender care they slowly put the starfish back in the crevice of its home.

As we slowly walked off the reef, the mist in the air caught the sun. A full rainbow stretched from the shore to sea, pulling my eye out to the world beyond.

Creatures of the Sea

The Maori consider the ocean to be the source and foundation of all essence. Many Maori still rely on the sea for sustenance to life. It is fundamental to the history of their religion, lifestyle and survival.

Being out of the city and living in a rural community I began to sense a desire to experience a deeper natural living that was possible in the wilds of New Zealand. Chad was feeling this as well and we began to seek out family adventures that would fill our stomachs as well as our spirits.

On a hot summer day, equipped with buckets, we drove to a well-known area in Mahia with flat sandy beaches where a small river flowed into the Pacific to dig for pipis, a shellfish similar to a clam. We waded waist-deep into the warm river as we watched the other hunters. I began wiggling my toes, searching for shells in the sandy bottom of the river. When I could feel their hard edges I would bend down and fill my hands. The sand would sift from my fingers, floating back to the riverbed, as I pulled the pipis towards the surface. Looking through my find I threw the small shells back into the river and dumped the larger ones in my bucket. Bending, grabbing and sifting. Quickly we filled our buckets and began to enjoy the water. Work turned to play. I floated down the river, pulled by the current. I wiggled my toes in the sun and laid my head back. Gazing at the sky, I floated lazily.

At home we dumped our treasure on the counter. A bit uncertain what to do we consulted the Internet. Chad took over and donning an apron, professionally steamed and prepared the pipis. We watched as the shells slowly bloomed open to reveal a small white meat. A well-earned, filling meal.

Reclining in our chairs the next day some friends from Sweden pulled up. Excitedly, Stephan directed us to the boot (otherwise known as the trunk) of his car where his wife Joanna was gazing in with pride. We stuck our heads in and saw a large stingray laying on a plastic bag. I'm sure our faces registered shock. Joanna had just pulled this creature out of the ocean while surfcasting on the beach in town. They had managed to get it into the trunk without being stung. We were quite impressed with this catch. They drove off promising to find out if it was edible.

Sure enough, later in the day Stephan returned with some filets of stingray, guaranteeing that according to a search of the great World Wide Web, the meat could indeed be eaten. Unsure of how to prepare the fillet I decided to add it to the remaining pipis and make a chowder. A little while later we were delighted to discover what a nice, flaky meat stingray has. The rich, creamy chowder reminded us of how close to the sea we were in every sense.

For two weeks each spring the whitebait run. Whitebait is a small, juvenile, freshwater fish. The larvae wash down the river and into the sea where they hatch and then swim back up the river as adults. The eggs are laid in the riverbank grasses in the fall during the flood season. The eggs hatch into larvae in the spring and tides flush them out into the sea. For six months they live in the ocean as part of the plankton mass. The juveniles then return to rivers and move upstream to live in freshwater.

As I ran along the river one beautiful spring morning, I noticed men sitting on the docks fishing for whitebait. Layered in t-shirts and jackets against the cool morning, caps covering their wizened heads, they had all the time in the world to spend fishing along the river. Some were alone enjoying the solitude, while others stood in groups and caught up on happenings around town. Jogging past, I felt the stillness. The men quietly dipped their long circular nets down into the water, let them skim the river for the tiny fish and pulled them out with small bits of silver wiggling and glittering in the sunlight. Every once in a while I passed a car with the door open and music floating out into the air. I turned away from the river and headed into town. My elderly friend Norm, from dance class, was passing by. We stopped to chat for a moment. He confided in me that it wasn't a good morning of fishing; he only got a handful of whitebait.

Stew gave me a container of whitebait over the fence one day. My family looked through the plastic at all the little eyes peering out at us. They were small and looked like slimy little worms. Everyone in town had been talking about fritters, so I decided to try cooking them. It's basically an omelet with fish in it. After a few bites, we got over being disturbed about eating the whole fish-skin, bones, tails and eyes—and began to enjoy our meal. They weren't too bad, but I can't say I will be ordering whitebait fritters off a menu any time soon.

Paua is considered a delicacy by the Maori. Known as "abalone" in other parts of the world, this sea snail is found in shallow coastal waters along rocky shorelines. They cling to the rocks with their muscular foot during tidal surges and feed on seaweed. Strict fishing guidelines protect them from extinction.

The Maori of Hawke's Bay often dive, in the traditional fashion, for paua. Camouflaged under a thick layer of algae, its shell is one of the most colorful of the abalone species. The shell radiates greens, pinks, purples and blues when polished. The Maori have used the shells in their native art for centuries. They regard it as a treasure from the god of the seas.

On a late summer day, Chad had the opportunity to go crayfish hunting with a co-worker. While I had the enjoyment of hanging out in their bach (summer cottage) in Mahia with his wife, Chad geared up for the dive. They headed down the peninsula about a mile to do a shore dive.

As Chad recounted, "A shore dive is when one parks away from the water, puts on lots of equipment (at the car), then lugs himself down to the surf and (if he survives) gets in and has a nice dive. The best part is not having a boat payment.

"So a crayfish is a Red Rock Lobster. Yeah, sounds much more appetizing that way, doesn't it? Anyway, it is legal to just go down to the bottom, poke your head into any deep, dark cave or under any giant rock on the seabed, and pull out a lobster if you can. It's the greatest. One benefit of putting your head into sea caves and rock crevices is that the wetsuit gets warm rather quickly. The traditional way to catch crayfish is with one's hand. I agree, it was bad enough with the crevices and stuff, but it's tradition. Well, you know what I always say—tradition, schmadition. Most people who care about their limbs use a tool. The guy I went with had a hollow metal rod with a steel cable running through it; stuck out the end was a loop of that cable. He pulls the near end, and the loop at the far end gets tighter. See how that works? It's not the cray we're defeating here, it's bad Mr Crevice. My diving partner says crayfish have got something going for them, they've been around for millions more years than us. Well, I've got two things to say to the crayfish: frontal lobe and opposable thumbs.

"After the looping comes the fighting the lobster into a bag under water. Later comes the dipping the lobster into melted butter, which is what one must focus very intently on whilst dragging the many pounds of equipment (strapped tightly to the body) out onto the rocks and up the beach to the car.

"Mainly, it's not terrifying at all and lobster tastes good, so I think I'll do it again. Lobster must be 54mm wide at the tail to keep, and the daily limit is six lobsters per person. Life, as they say, is tough."

My men are tough, from diving for lobster to stabbing a kina.

Dive School

I was very proud of myself when I came up with the perfect birthday gift for Chad. Keeping in mind our future return to the States with more stuff, I wanted something that was distinct and unique to our experience and something that he would actually want without taking up much space or weighing much. Knowing his love for the water I checked into dive classes and certification. This had been a dream of his since our honeymoon when we took a little Club Med teaser course in Cancun. I distinctly remember being handed a banana by our instructor and told to feed it to the tropical fish. While trying to orient myself underwater, and not paying attention to the banana, a fish came, bit the banana—and took a bite of me in the process. Although the wound inflicted was minor, I wasn't keen on heading into that claustrophobic situation again. Chad, one the other hand, had loved it.

The first shop in Napier I called was perfect. They had a two-weekend class coming up with a special bonus—buy one get one free. The present was getting better by the moment, Damon could do the certification with him. It would be a perfect father and son bonding time.

Chad was quite pleased when I told him and talked it up a bit with the docs in town. Another one of the temporary doctors approached Chad and said, "Diving has been one of my goals for my year in New Zealand. Could Kris sign me up too?" Now I faced a dilemma. I picked up her money and quietly mumbled that there was a buy-one-get-one-free deal. What would she like me to do? "Kris, you can be my free person!" she said with glee. I was stuck now. Who can turn down three for the price of one? Especially when this was supposed to be the most magnificent gift ever for my husband. Thus was the beginning of my diving career.

The first weekend constituted of pool and classroom time. Being a responsible student, I read the book before arriving at the first class. The videos were a breeze. Day two began in the pool.

We were paired up—three dads with their three twelve year old sons; my partner who was not really comfortable with the water and overweight, but had a goal of becoming an instructor; and our friend Jackie. Jackie is an amazing and inspiring person. A survivor of brain cancer, her goal was to live life to the fullest, embrace every opportunity and fulfill every dream while she still had the opportunity.

The first exercise was simple. Go to the bottom of the pool and sit on the bottom until everyone was situated, then the instructor would begin leading us through the exercises. It was a disaster. We all began sinking to the twelve-foot bottom. Blowing my brains out with my nose pinched, I focused on getting my ears to pop and equilibrium established.

I made it to the bottom and sat cross-legged. My partner went up with some problem. The boys were in various states of panic and bobbed up and down while their dads followed trying to calm them down. Jackie became very uncomfortable with the feeling of all the gear and panicked. So there I sat on the bottom watching everyone go up and down while the instructors scrambled to gain some semblance of control.

I do not like closed in places. If Chad flips the covers over my face while getting in bed, I panic and claw the thin sheet from my face. We laugh over the silliness, but as I sat on the bottom of the pool I was faced with a mental battle. Soon the distraction of my classmates faded from my mind as I focused on breathing in and out. Just breathe, in and out, in and out... Eight hours on the bottom of the pool with only a break for lunch and a few changes of air tanks felt like a million years. Somehow we all managed to make it through that day. I climbed into the car for the ride home. Exhausted, we drove silently in the dark over the hills, around the bends and curves to home.

The next weekend came all too quickly. I took the written exam, finished the pool exercises, then helped load the gear into a van and drove out to the seashore. It was a windy day early in spring. The water was cold, the bay choppy. I pulled on my wetsuit, bent over and laid the weights on my back, cinching them tight around my waist. I checked my air, and struggled into my bcd. With masks pulled down, my partner and I faced each other and went through our pre-dive check.

I was ready to go. Taking a deep breath and focusing mentally, I waddled out to the water, my flippers making it difficult to walk on the tiny volcanic pebbles that made up the beach. The waves pulled at my feet. I struggled to stay standing as I continued to stagger forward. Eventually I realized it was easier to just sink to my knees, let the waves rush over me and be pulled out into the ocean. Breathing through my regulator, I paddled out to the meeting point. As each wave rolled over me I spotted my goal—Chad and Damon bobbing in the distance.

Eventually our class grouped together and was given the signal to go down. Face to face with my partner, we descended through the murky water to the ocean floor. We quickly found that we had to stay practically on top of each other because visibility was less than three feet. My only goal at this point was to make it down, stay under for thirty minutes to make it an official dive, and come back up again to the glorious open air. We went through our exercises holding tight to one another's wrists while being bashed against the coral in the choppy current.

Finally I swam to the surface. I had made it. I was still alive! I paddled in to shore, letting the surf carry me as much as possible. For a moment I became one with the waves breaking into the shore. Then they betrayed me. The ocean bashed me into the gravel then picked me up and bashed me again. The weight of the belt and tank was almost too much to bear. I clawed my way up the beach on my hands and knees until I became free of the sea and collapsed onto my back.

My instructor helped me get my gear off and wrapped a towel around me.

"We're over for the day. The sea is too rough to do our second dive."

Duh...

I lay awake that night in my hotel bed, haunted by the darkness of the ocean and the waves tossing me around like a rubber ducky.

I awoke and prepared to complete my last two dives. This time we headed to a much more sheltered bay, but I took one look at the water and lost it. I hit a mental barricade like a car slamming into a brick wall. I was trying to walk through the wall of water God provided for the Israelites rather than on the path He opened.

"I can't do it." I looked into Chad's eyes, pleading with him.

"No problem." And like that, relief washed over me. I sat on the rocks, hugging my knees close as Chad and Damon got into the water. But the disaster was not over. They paddled out and while waiting for the rest of the group, Damon's bcd failed; it would not hold air. Frantically trying to stay above water with all the additional weight, his flipper came off. He panicked. The instructor grabbed him and dragged him ashore. Feeling Damon's hands the instructor said, "He's too cold, he needs to get out of the water." So shivering under towels, we huddled on shore as Chad completed his dives.

Oddly, this failure in life didn't bother me as some do. I was very comfortable with *when the going got tough the wimps bailed out.* It was a hard point to come to; one that I had battled with all night long.

A few months later summer came. Damon and I returned to Napier on a brilliant, sunny day. This time the ocean was calm. The sky reflected on the water as if it was a mirror. We returned to the same bay we had so miserably failed at before. As we sank below the surface of the sea a Water Duck boat filled with Asian tourists passed. Cameras clicked, people waved at us. Apparently we were the newest attraction in Napier. With ten feet visibility and no current we quickly completed our two dives.

While we were sitting on the rocks in our wet suits our Maori guide came over, his dive knife in one hand and a prickly kina in the other. He stabbed it and handed it to Damon. The sea urchin of New Zealand is an important traditional food to the Maori. He told Damon to pour it in his mouth and without hesitation, Damon did. I was proud of my son but relieved that I was not offered one as well.

I was elated with my diving certificate and was told over and over that I would never experience a dive as horrendous as I did on that day in

Napier. Now each time I sit on the edge of a boat, ready to fall backwards into the water, I hold onto that promise.

Dive HQ
http://www.divehq.co.nz

Morere Hot Springs

A walk in the woods breathes life into me. Getting away from the house, the cement, the daily grind of life and onto a dirt trail secluded by jungle with streams bubbling along carrying water from a place deep in the earth out to the sea refreshes me to the innermost parts of my being.

About forty minutes from Wairoa on the way north to Gisborne, we discovered Morere Hot Springs. It's a bit off the beaten tourist track so the feeling of having found a place on this earth that is one's own hangs over the park. This gem is located on 365 hectares of pristine lowland rainforest. Rainforest was the key word for me. Upon entering I stepped into another world full of lush vegetation where I felt dwarfed like a Smurfette walking out of her mushroom house into the enormous outdoors. The lush stands of Nikau Palms were striking as I hiked through the remaining forest that once covered the coast. The Nikau is native to this area and only found on the mainland of New Zealand. Giant trees stretch towards the sky while dense undergrowth of vines, ferns, shrubs and orchids fight for space. Walking tracks snaked through the reserve up and down hills, along ridges, and over streams. We wandered along the paths, over rocks and next to the stream. We found a vine for the kids to swing on. They shouted like Tarzan full of freedom and adventure. The girls crawled into a hollow log that begged to be explored. Over the time we lived in New Zealand we eventually wandered all of Morere's paths. From the Ridge Track we gazed upon farmlands and forests stretching out forever before us while the Mangakawa Track took us past waterfalls and gorges.

A fifteen-minute walk down the Nikau Pools Track brought us to hot springs. A small changing area gave us privacy while we prepared to enter the pools. To be honest, the water was a bit murky although it was cleaned regularly. The minerals gave a slippery coating to my skin as I slid into the water. It's not the "chlorine clean" feeling given by pools I was used to swimming in. Relaxing in the water, the weariness from hiking faded away. The natural heat of the water warmed my body on a chilly day. The Maori used the springs to wash in long before the Europeans discovered the pools. Bathers have been coming to the springs to find healing and relaxation in the mineral pools since the 1890's. In the 20's and 30's the area became a popular tourist spot with hotels and spas piping the mineral water to bathhouses. Eventually a fire and landslides destroyed the original structures. There are eight pools in all and two can be rented as private plunging pools. We welcomed the cold swimming pool on a hot summer day.

Hamburgers on the barbecue in the park topped off the day. When I think of a grill in America, I think of a grate with fire from a source below. In New Zealand "fried" is the word of choice, therefore the grills are stainless steel sheets with a gas source below. If McDonald's is your cup of tea then you will feel at home here, but if you are a flame broiled Burger King fan then kiss your dreams of a good cookout goodbye while in New Zealand.

Morere Hot Springs
3968 State Highway 2, Morere
http://www.morerehotsprings.co.nz/index.html

<u>Gisborne</u>

About once a month Chad would pop at the seams.

"I need some civilization, some city!"

So we would pile into the car and settle in for a drive to the "city." Gisborne is one hour and fifteen minutes north of Wairoa. It was the lesser of the two evils. The road to Napier had more hills and curves. We could make the drive to Gisborne without anyone becoming carsick and losing their breakfast out the window. Because of the distance these trips tended to be full day outings.

For seventy-five minutes I would lean back in my chair as we drove along lazy roads with stretches of ocean in view. With the window cracked, fresh sea air would thread its fingers through my hair. Sheep dotted the green, rolling countryside. Quaint homes on farms passed by, peaceful and restful. As we approached Gisborne the scenery would change to vineyards with sheep grazing amongst grapevines.

Gisborne is the third largest grape-growing region in the country. Known as the "Chardonnay Capital of New Zealand," they also produce Gewurztraminer, Viognier and Chenin Blanc wines. A wine trail map will guide you to many vineyards and boutique wineries for samplings and dining.

Tradition says that *Kaiti Beach* is where the Horouta canoe brought the first Maori to the area. It is also where the first Europeans set foot in New Zealand. On October 8, 1769 Nicholas Young, the twelve year old surgeon's assistant, was the first on board the *Endeavour* to spot land. The rugged white cliffs at the southern tip of the bay rose out of the sea calling the ship near. As a reward to the young hand, the cliffs were named *Young Nicks Head*. They sailed into the bay and the crew, in desperate need of supplies, stepped ashore. Captain Cook took his men across the river and walked along the Waikanae Stream. They left gifts near some Maori homes. Hearing gunfire, Cook quickly turned back and found that a Maori had been killed while warning shots were fired. The next day the locals challenged the landing party with the Haka. With neither side understanding the customs of the other, people were killed and Cook fled without the supplies so needed. In frustration Cook named the area *Poverty Bay*,"...as it afforded us not one thing we wanted."

Grand palm trees line the medium as you enter on Gladstone Road. A slow, beach town feeling makes Gisborn a great place to spend the day. This small town of 35,000 people claims more sunny days than anywhere else in New Zealand. It grows in population during the summer as surfers flock in to hit the waves.

The Maori name for Gisborne is *Taira Whiti* which means "the coast upon which the sun shines across the water."[4] Being the first city in the world to see the sun each day, the name still fits. Every year 30,000 people flock to Waiohika Estate to party the New Year in. Bands perform for three days culminating in the sun rising over the ocean and green hills to be the first city to welcome a New Year to the world.

Gladstone Road is lined with shops and restaurants. Window-shopping while sipping a coffee or licking an ice cream cone blew an hour and made us feel civilized. I never got over giggling at the relaxed dress of some locals. Strolling down the street in nylon—a bit too short—shorts, rugby shirt and gum boots, the practical attire made a fashion statement of its own!

Edwardian style churches pulled me in for a peek. I sat in a pew on a quiet afternoon, the sun shining through the stained glass windows. The rays sprayed color around the sanctuary and I felt the peace of God surround me. I loved the charming architecture and colorful facades. Old wooden doors with heavy wrought iron hardware complemented the red brick.

A favorite church of mine was at the base of *Kaiti Hill.* A drive up the ridge leads to a spectacular overlook of Poverty Bay. Just outside James Cook Observatory at the top of the hill is a nice clearing with picnic tables. The view was worth braving the breeze and holding onto our lunch.

In the summer two options for beaches provided a respite from the heat. Located on the north end of Poverty Bay, *Kaiti Beach* is calm and protected. A statue of Cook marks the spot where he first brought his crew ashore. Families flock there to cool off on a hot day. The Taruneru and Waimate Rivers flow through town then join and pour into the north end of Poverty Bay. Barges loaded with logs come in through the channel on the east side of the river. The beach is on the west. With shipping traffic and multitudes of people, this bay felt a bit dirty to me.

My favorite beach, *Makarori Point,* is located ten minutes north of town. Also a favorite among surfers, the area is known for great waves. A stretch of soft, yellow sand as far as the eye can see was a welcome relief to the black lava pebbles of many other New Zealand beaches. After watching the surfers spin their boards on the waves for a while, we would grab our boogie boards and run into the aqua blue sea. Life felt endless. We screamed in delight, laughing together as we played for a few hours then collapsed on the beach to enjoy the view. As the sun began to sink, we collected our things and headed back into town for dinner.

New Zealand seems like an odd place to fall in love with Indian food, but while we looked for a change from the typical bland cuisine, we stumbled upon *Preet Indian Tandori.* Restaurant-style vinyl and metal chairs circled the tables. Woven fabrics were protected by thick plastic tablecloths. We sat on vinyl chairs while Bollywood videos entertained us. Lost in the unrealistic romance of wealthy Indians, we would join in with the popular hand motions. The flamboyant style and culture added extra flavor and a smile to our garlic naan and butter chicken.

As the sun began to set on the sea, we piled back into the car for the ride home. Stomachs full of good food, sea salt in our hair and memories of a day in the city to sustain us for awhile rested in our minds as we drove home in silence.

Preet Indian Tandori
55 Gladstone Rd.

Tairawhiti Museum
Kelvin Park, Stout St.
This museum is known as one of the best regional museums in New Zealand. Exhibits depict ancient and current histories of the region.
http://www.tairawhitimuseum.org.nz/about-us/defaultasp.asp

Te Moana Maritime Museum and SS Star of Canada
10 Stout St.
A unique opportunity to learn about maritime myths, legends and stories. Study the history of James Cook and explore the steamship SS Star.

East Coast Museum of Technology
67 Main Rd.
A display of historic artifacts from the area, focusing on technology.
http://www.ecmot.org.nz/

Rhythm and Vines Festival
http://rhythmandvines.co.nz/

Eastwoodhill Arboretum

Mark Twain said, "Truth is stranger than fiction, but it is because Fiction is obliged to stick to possibilities; Truth isn't." Eccentric people who do great things color our world with "stranger than fiction" stories. The founder of Eastwoodhill Arboretum was one such person.

William Douglas Cook established a farm in 1910, naming it *Eastwoodhill* after his mother's family farm near Glasgow. He immediately began creating a garden with trees, flowers, shrubs and vegetables. He volunteered to serve in the army during the First World War and in France he lost the sight of his right eye. While recovering with family in Scotland, he was inspired by the English style gardens. When he returned to Eastwoodhill in 1918, Cook began planting thousands of Monterey Pine trees from California for wood production and firewood.

He also planted White Gum and Camden Woollybutt from Australia. Soon after, he created parkland and imported a greater varieties of trees.

After traveling again to Europe he extended his garden with tulips, hyacinths and peonies from the Netherlands. Passionate about trees, he soon began to develop parks throughout his property.

Visitors heard of the gardens but they learned that they must call ahead to see the property so as not to be surprised by a rather naked Cook. An enthusiastic nudist, he wore only one gumboot to help with digging holes while gardening. He invested all his money in the gardens. With his health failing and out of money, Cook sold the property in 1965.

Today Eastwoodhill is home to the largest collection of Northern Hemisphere trees in the Southern Hemisphere. One hundred thirty five hectares of hills with valleys, ponds and walking trails create a unique forest and gardens.

Thinking of spring back home in the States while experiencing fall in New Zealand was a bit disorienting. To lift our spirits we decided to visit the arboretum located just twenty-two miles from Gisborne. The North Island is considered a sub-tropical region. We were surprised to see palm trees growing in town. It was hard to feel "fall" with no change in the color of the leaves. Walking through the hills of the arboretum, we thrilled at the blazing reds and oranges of the deciduous trees as they were preparing for winter. We delighted in discovering bright red mushrooms snuggled in fallen leaves. The earthy smell of fresh dirt along a path through the woods felt just like a fall walk back home.

Eastwoodhill Arboretum
www.eastwoodhill.blogspot.com

Rere Rock Slide

After we left the Arboretum we wanted to check out a rockslide that we had heard was another ten miles up the road. Driving along Wharekopae Rd. we came upon the beautiful Rere Waterfall. Waterfalls are my passion and I will drag the family down long walking trails if there is hope of a waterfall at the end.

I sat on the edge of the Wharekopae River and dangled my feet in the cool water. Although the waterfall is only sixteen feet in height, the sixty-six foot length made it feel grand. Soon Chad and Damon were in the water paddling around. They swam up to the falls, walked under the cascade and jumped in through the falls.

As I wandered around I noticed apples lying on the ground. I looked up the cliff and saw two apple trees clinging to the edge.

After the swim we found our way around the ledge and up to the two trees near the road. But there was a problem. Untethered cows grazed on the grass under the trees. Not having much keenness for small animals, large animals really put me on edge. But I really wanted those apples. Like a baby crawling for candy, I crept toward the trees. While keeping one eye on those lazy brown cow eyes I plucked apples off the tree and threw them into my bag. Every time a cow shifted its weight I recalculated the distance between me, the car and the cliff. Of course my fearless family was throwing apples into their bags faster than a picking machine.

Triumphantly we placed our overflowing bags of apples into the trunk and continued our search for the rockslide.

At the slide we put on our "must have in New Zealand" water shoes, grabbed our boogie boards and walked down the short trail to the river. A delightful sight opened before us. A giant natural water slide on a rock face was made smooth by the continual rush of the river dumping into a pool two hundred feet away. Moss swaying in the current created a lubricant that promised to make our boards fly unhindered by friction. There were no lifeguards enforcing unwanted rules, no obnoxious fences or warning signs. To be sure none of us would die, I let Chad try it out first. He ran and belly-flopped onto his board; with whoops and hollers he flew down the rock face. The kids were fast on his heels. With space for us all I tentatively pushed myself off. Gaining speed I flew toward the calm pool below. Unexpectedly my board turned around. I couldn't see where I was going and completely freaked out. My squeals quickly turned into high-pitched screams. Being a person who likes complete control at all times, my arms and legs began flailing wildly. With my heart pounding I hit the pool at the bottom and slowed down. My husband and kids watched me, laughing much too hard to head up the natural path along the edge. With a feeling of elation I ran up the path, passed them and this time used the running belly-flop method. We continued until we were too tired to stand on our legs any longer.

This is one of the things that I love about New Zealand, finding natural ways to have immense amounts of fun and adventure.

We munched on apples during our ride home, savoring their sweet, pink flesh. Those apples turned out to make the best homemade applesauce I have ever tasted—another rewarding product of New Zealand.

Rere Rockslide
50 Km from Gisborne on the Wharekopae Rd. towards Eastwoodhill Arboretum

Homemade Applesauce
By Kristen Faber

Peel, core and slice apples.

Fill a roasting pan 3/4 full of apples. Add enough water to cover bottom so apples don't burn. Place in 350° F oven. Stir every 30 minutes until apples are falling apart.

Remove from oven and stir until sauce is desired consistency.

Add sugar and cinnamon to taste or a family favorite is to use Red Hot Candies to give a little snap to the sauce.

Cool.

Freeze in containers.

Lake Waikaremoana

Te Urewera National Park

Have you ever had a day or an experience that you felt was simply a gift from God? A moment that was so special you knew you hadn't done anything to earn or deserve it, God was just smiling at you, asking you to enjoy His gift to its fullest?

Let me tell you about a day like that. My husband was the official doctor for the first *Lake to Lighthouse* adventure race. It began an hour away in the mountains and ended the next day in Wairoa. The *Coast to Coast* race on the South Island has long been a famous, highly sought after adventure race. Now the *Lake to Lighthouse* race brings in athletes from all over the world as well. The race has been revamped and the new *Genesis Energy Lake Waikaremoana Challenge* is "...renowned for its organization, social and cultural qualities and the sheer challenge of being NZ's toughest multi-sport event the past four years." according to adventurerace.com. It is the only adventure race that focuses on Maori culture and hospitality.

The original race began at Lake Waikaremoana and finished the next day at the Lighthouse in Wairoa. The race has been changed to focus on the Lake Wairkaremoana area with one and two day races for individuals and teams. The two-day challenge covers 137km and comprises mountain biking, trail running and kayaking.

I decided to go up for the day to help out with whatever needed doing. I arranged for the kids to spend the night with friends and had just cozied up to the computer when the phone rang. Ruth asked if I would like to ride up to the race in the helicopter with her. Russell has the uber cool job of flying a helicopter. He was going to be doing air support and video coverage for the race.

At 4:30 the next morning, Ruth and Russell picked me up. We headed to the hangar and climbed up into the helicopter. I had never been in a helicopter before. As we went up, my grip began to relax and the peace of the darkness surrounding us washed over me. We flew into Tui, then Russell turned the helicopter around. A glorious sunrise came up over the mountains. We paused a moment to take in the splendor of it all then we descended into the fog below. I hopped out and ran over to Chad where he was waiting for us. We got coffee and watched the race begin. The race was well staffed with volunteers so Ruth and I were not needed. We decided to catch a water taxi to the other side of the lake to cheer for the runners as they passed a checkpoint. For thirty minutes we skimmed across the waters of Lake Waikaremoana, the wind whipping our hair and the sun smiling down on us.

Lake Waikaremoana is located in *Te Urewera National Park,* the third largest of fourteen national parks in New Zealand. Located at the northeast end of Hawkes Bay, the park covers 2,127 sq. km of primeval rainforest. To get there you must be prepared to drive on some shingle (gravel) roads. I found this out the hard way when driving a nine-passenger van up a hill on a two lane road and had a flat tire!

The park is located in the heart of *Tuhoe* country. The *Tuhoe* reacted to destructive forays into their area by the government in the early 1870's by isolating themselves and closing off access to their lands. Today the *Tuhoe* still have a reputation for a strong adherence to their Maori identity and the use of the Maori language. They became known as "The

Children of the Mist" when Elsdon Best wrote an in-depth, two volume survey of the Maori culture by that title.

Another friend who is an EMT was also headed to the checkpoint to help with emergencies. Ian told us about a waterfall that was a short hike from the drop off point. When we landed we knew we had about two hours before the first racer would come through, so Ruth and I decided to hike up to the waterfall. We walked through stunning rainforest and jumped from rock to rock to get across rivers and streams. At a corner we turned and our breath was taken away by the view of the water cascading before us. Veering off the trail and climbing down rocks, we got as close to the bottom as possible. We sat down on a large rock, and with the mist from the waterfall dampening our skin, we ate a few oranges picked off the tree that morning, and soaked in the beauty.

After hiking back, we sat and cheered for the racers as they passed by. Eventually it was time to catch another boat for the thirty-minute ride across the lake. The wind blew in my face while mountains flew by. We arrived in time to enjoy a snack before the first racer crossed the finish line on his bike. After we watched several more finish, Russell announced that he was done and ready to head out.

Leaving Chad behind, I followed Ruth into the helicopter and we headed out over the countryside for Russell to do another quick job for a farmer before we headed home. New Zealand is beautiful from the air. As Wairoa came into view, I was taken aback by the loveliness of the town surrounded by hills, a river winding into it on one side and the ocean crashing on the other. By 5:00 I was back home with the kids, but not quite ready to let go of the special day. We picked up some fish and chips, went down to the river to eat and then popped in a movie as we waited for Chad to come home.

I found the area enchanting and made it to Lake Waikaremoana several times over the year. Ruth and Russell took us on our first trip. We did a portion of the three to four day *Lake Waikaremoana Great Walk.* This is considered one of the best scenic walks in New Zealand. The trail follows the edge of the lake in a remote region of the country. This twenty-eight mile track will take you through dense native rainforest, past spectacular geological formations, abundant birdlife, magnificent rivers, and waterfalls, and through ghostly valleys of mist. One might see small Maori tribes that still live in the forest.

Nine walks comprise the Great Walks of New Zealand. These well-maintained trails cut through the most rugged and beautiful scenery the country has to offer. No fees or permits are needed for day hiking but if you want to spend the night in the backcountry or huts along the way, you must make a reservation ahead of time.

We walked across suspension bridges and followed paths cut into the sides of the mountains as we wound our way along part of the lake. We traveled through many different eco-systems and marveled at the tall grasses in the fields and ferns unfolding in the dense forest. At lunchtime we found ourselves on a beautiful sandy beach near the Puketukutuku Peninsula at the edge of the Kiwi conservation reserve. Propped against driftwood, I let my mind wander. I enjoyed every moment of the present with new friends but also thought of friends back home who would have loved to be there with me at that moment on that beach. There were so many times I wished I could intertwine my old life and new, my old friends and new.

Being more aware of my senses in the wilderness, I listened to the sound of the winds across the lake and through the trees. Various birds sang out to one another. Russell commented on the type. I love to watch large, graceful birds there is a quiet strength in their size yet a gentleness in their beauty. In Michigan, I was often entranced by herons as they silently strutted in the water, fishing for their dinner. As I gazed out on the lake, I noticed a family of black swans. A mother and father with six cygnets. There was a stunning elegance to them as they floated on the glassy lake. They were introduced to New Zealand from Australia as a game bird. A black swan would be very rare in Michigan, yet I had not seen a single white swan in New Zealand. "That's because the queen owns them all!" Ruth said.

It was time to move on. We turned down the trail to head back to the car. We soon found that life is always an adventure with Russell. "I'm pretty sure I saw a short-cut from the helicopter when I was over here the other day," he commented as we came to a fork in the trail. We followed our trusty leader down the path. Eventually we came to a good-sized river flowing over the rocks. With shoes off and pants pulled up, we followed him into the river. About half way across, my feet were numb with cold and I was hobbling along the rocky river bed. The spring snowmelt was frigid. Despite the squealing, we made it across the river, up a steep path and to our car. With my feet tucked close to the heater, I gazed at another waterfall along the road. Whether on a path or in the car, *Te Urewera National Park* entrances one in the beauty it holds.

On a school camp trip with Maddie's class I experienced the park in a completely different way. Throughout the park, boxes are nailed to trees at eye level. They have a hinged door that can be opened to observe the weta in the wild.

A weta is a large cricket-like creature with a wingspan of up to seven inches. This makes it the world's largest insect. Like a cockroach on steroids, it is really quite disgusting. With spiny hind legs, beady eyes and antennae sticking out of their heads, they are able to bite and claw in defense. Ok, so typically they just run away or crawl into a crack, but they *are* scary enough to give me nightmares.

The plan was to explore the Onepoto caves around the lake on this particular school trek. "Caves" must be said with care because in reality these were large limestone rocks that formed tunnels along the cliffs when an upheaval of the land formed the lake long ago.

We tramped down the trail as a group, careful not to slip on the wet ground. When we came to the first cave, we looked in. The trail went straight down into complete darkness. Chatter about the cave wetas living down there excited the children. The guide, a big Maori man, looked at me and said, "You go first." Little did he know about my fear of enclosed spaces. Little did he know about my fear of seven-inch insects. I lay on the ground and dangled my feet over the edge, feeling for firm footing. Slowly I found a rock and moved down a bit more. I closed out the whines of impatient kids above and continued down. Eventually I could not see where I was going any longer and full-blown panic took hold of me. Some boys from the class began to push forward saying they would lead the way. At this point I was too far into panic mode to have any concern for the young innocents around me. I clawed my way first over Maddie, then over the group of children headed down. Stepping on hands and knees, I found my way to the top and tossed over my shoulder, "I'll meet you back at camp." and hastily continued on my way. I walked for awhile, trying to calm my shaking hands and slow my breathing. About the time I had myself under control, I realized that I had absolutely no idea where I was.

Fortunately I was on a trail and I realized that I would eventually either come out by the lake or on a road. After wandering some more, I came to State Highway 38, made a turn and took the very long way back to camp. As I arrived in the parking lot the other mums ran up to me and said, "We were just dividing into search parties to look for you." Lovely. Lesson learned. Don't panic, keep your head about you and don't wander off into the wilderness alone.

Lake Waikaremoana - visitor information
www.waikaremoana.com

Genesis Energy Lake Waikaremoana Challenge – race information
www.laketolighthouse.co/nz

Rain of the Children - A film documenting the history of a bride, Puhi, a Maori prophet, and her schizophrenic son. The story illustrates the life of the Maori and the Tuhoe history.

Sports

Part of the adventure of living halfway across the world was to experience the sports that people played and faithfully followed but were unfamiliar to us. To understand a people, you must understand their games. The kids had opportunities galore to learn new games. We found most New Zealand sports similar to American sports, only with a bit of a twist.

Saturday nights found my boys at our friend Gail's house watching rugby. A true fan, she wore a jersey, drank tea and had complete faith that the All Blacks, the national team, would win. It wasn't long before our family became die-hard All Backs fans as well and found our way to a test (an unofficial, but widely used term for international games) in Wellington.

Prior to the test we put on tattoos and face paint to show some national pride. The game against the South African Springboks, a major rival, was sold out despite the cold rain.

The pre-game entertainment was opera. I'm not really sure how well that would have gone over in America, but as the concert was going on they brought two huge flags onto the field and the teams entered. The South African national anthem was sung in Afrikaans and then English, followed by the New Zealand national anthem sung in Maori then English. I felt far removed from Michigan with many languages swirling in my mind.

Next the All Blacks put some fear into South Africa with the Haka. South Africa stood facing New Zealand, quaking in their shoes, as the All Blacks did their war dance ending with their faces contorted and tongues hanging from their mouths. This instilled trepidation in the Springboks, then suddenly, without warning, the test was in play. Similar to but very different from, American football, I tried to equate every move with something I had seen before.

Within minutes the first, what I call "WWF Move," happened. A New Zealand guy picked up a South African, flipped him over and threw him backside onto the ground! The referees conferred and decided it was legal.

Another move is when the refs aren't really sure whose ball it is so both teams go into what I call the "tackle dummy" position. Each team makes three short rows facing each other only inches apart, head to head and ready to plow one another over. Then another smallish guy timidly tosses the ball under this huddle between the two teams. He literally turns and hightails it out of there to the back of the pile so that he won't get crushed. It is a toss up as to which team will win the ball.

My personal favorite move is what I call the "cheerleader lift." When the ball goes out of bounds, each team hoists a man into the air in an effort to catch the ball. Two men fly up with grace and come down— sometimes caught by a teammate and other times not.

Quite frequently there is the "greased pig" move. The ball is passed around a lot, confusing the opponent, but then they finally figure out which guy to tackle. Guys from both sides pile on top of the man carrying the ball. Punches fly and the next thing you know the ball has reappeared from under the pile and is in play again. They all run after this new guy and pile on top of him, the ball reappears again and play continues. This is a bit like the "clumping method" of soccer seen when four year old kids play.

Last we have the "slip and slide" play when the guy with the ball dives to the ground and slides ten yards to make a "try" (goal).

Oh, did I mention that they do all this without helmets and pads? Incredible!

I came to enjoy this game a lot as it is quick, with the ball continually in motion zig-zagging around the field. There are no time-outs with forty minutes in each half. Just throw the boys in the backyard and let them have at it!

Elena decided to try her hand at Netball. It is very similar to basketball with a few differences. Truly an all girls sport, the game is played in a skirt. The court is similar to a basketball court with a hoop at each end. Despite the name "netball," there is no net on the ring and no backboard. There are seven players on the court. Players don't bounce the ball, rather, it's a game of quick passing to teammates. Players have positions which restrict where she is able to move on the court and who is able to shoot for goals. As with all kid's sports, the play was a bit slow and the girls a bit confused, but through the experience we picked up the rules to the game along with a few new friends.

The English sport of cricket is similar to baseball. The games are tediously long, sometimes lasting for days. My neighbor, Stew, would watch for hours with nothing happening. Typically when he got up to greet me at the door a good play would happen and runs would be made. He would return to his chair only to sit for hours with nothing more to see.

A paddle-like bat is used to whack the ball so that the batting team can score runs. The field is a large rectangle of grass with a hard-packed earth pitch in the center.

One player from the other team acts as a pitcher but is called the "bowler." He "bowls" the ball, bouncing it once on the ground before the batsman hits it. The batsman then runs around the wickets carrying his bat. There seemed to be a lot of rules on making runs and getting out. This game is one that takes patience and dedication to watch. I never had enough of either to actually understand it.

In college my husband and I would occasionally grab our rackets and head to a court for a game of racquetball. Damon picked up the Southern Hemisphere equivalent with a neighbor friend. Our little town had a club with a nice set of squash courts. Squash is the older game with more history. The small, dense squash ball explodes with energy when hit then slows as the volley continues. The racket has a longer handle and a smaller, round head that makes it look more like a badminton racket. The court has lines and boxes for out-of-bound and serving areas. Although the rules and plays are a bit different, it's easy to move from one sport to the other if your part of the world demands it.

We were disappointed to find soccer largely lacking in New Zealand. We had assumed that when you left the US, life revolved around soccer. Not so. What we did find was that field hockey was very popular with plenty of opportunities. The girls decided to try out the sport. Having grown up on an ice rink in Michigan with hockey pucks flying around, I had a bit of an understanding of the game. Field hockey brought back great memories of nights living in Detroit as the Red Wings won the

Stanley Cup. What a good time to give this new sport a try. The field, positions and strategy are similar to soccer, so we had a basic knowledge going in.

The history of field hockey goes all the way back to 200 BC with a hockey-like game played in Greece. For 1,000 years the Chinese have been playing a similar game called beikou. In 1363, Edward III of England issued a proclamation using for the first time the word "hockey." English public schools refined the game in the 1800's, with the modern rules having been set in place by a cricket club.

Mainly an outside sport played on grass, the field is set up similarly to a soccer field. Eleven players on each team attempt to hit the ball into the net to score a point. As the players run up and down the field, they have their stick in their hands and an eye on the fast moving ball.

The game is enjoyable and quick moving. There is never a dull moment. The girls happily spent fall mornings in practice and play.

Because in New Zealand there is water near at hand wherever you are, water sports are very popular. Watching the Olympics reminds me how strong New Zealand is in rowing, wind surfing and sailing. The seas and rivers flow through a Kiwi's veins like life-giving blood. In the summer months people flood to the water for relaxation. Each town has local clubs to bring people together to enjoy the sports.

We love kayaking on the rivers of Michigan, so rowing was a natural fit for Maddie. She practiced at the local rowing club during the winter. It was a relaxing way to spend the evening rowing on the machines. This gave her a feel to the rhythm of the boat and a chance to build her strength. In the spring they got the boats out and she had opportunities to glide down the peaceful river. A long, wide and straight stretch of water is necessary in rowing. The Wairoa River was ideal, pulling in clubs from other towns.

The local sailing club was alive and active in teaching and competing. The clubhouse showcased black and white photos and old trophies giving a strong sense of history to the sport.

The kids and I signed up for beginning sailing. Each Saturday morning we headed down to the river to help take out the boats. We learned how to assemble the sails, tie the ropes and get the boats into the water.

Practicing first on land before putting the boats in the water, we learned how to make the boat go where we wanted. This of course was theory and never worked in reality. The kids caught on much quicker than I did. In the middle of the river, I tended to spend most of my morning spread-eagle on the bottom of the boat. The boom would swing back and forth and the only way to avoid being hit in the head was to duck, dive or just stay down. Every once in a while I would peek over the edge as I heard one of the kids yell, "Mom, turn the rudder!" I would take their advice, be knocked in the head and end up once more in the bottom of the boat.

Sailing presented many concepts that I just couldn't seem to grasp such as: wind, currents, sails, centerboards and rudders. You need to grow up with these ideas for them to become second nature or have an inborn instinct guiding you. Eventually the instructor would make her way over to me in the motorboat, get me sorted out and I would be on my way once again toward that eternally out of reach goal—the orange buoy. Five minutes later I would be a tangled mess and on the bottom of the boat.

Eventually I progressed so that I could sort-of make it around the three buoys in the river while my kids did loops around me and encouraged me on. I was very happy to see my photo in the local paper, proudly holding my certificate with a passel of little kids.

I have a new respect for the wind, the sea and those who sail on it.

Another way to spend a lazy weekend day in the summer was with the waterski club. Members came from as far as Napier to take advantage of the straight, wide river. Pulling their boats over the mountain passes, around tight curves and up hills, they camped out in Wairora for a long weekend. They were excited to share the sport with anyone who was willing to put on skis and jump in the river.

After a daylong clinic the kids began to improve quickly. They moved from holding on to a pole sticking out the side of the boat, to the rope on the back, and eventually on to the wakeboard. I loved riding in the boat, flying across the surface of the water, cheering my kids on.

Sunburned and exhausted, we would throw our towels around our necks and lazily walk home for dinner on the grill.

Rotorua

Rotorua, the Yellowstone of New Zealand, is located in the heart of the North Island. An area with many geothermal attractions, Maori culture and outdoor activities, it is a major tourist hub. We made several trips there during our year because we loved the get-away and it was a definite must-do on our list when company came to visit.

Because of the extreme geothermal activity in the area, Elena would hold her nose for the entire weekend. The smell of rotten eggs in the air is not subtle, and for this little girl it was unbearable. The earth seemed to bubble beneath my feet everywhere I went.

The more rustic camping lodges at Rotorua Thermal Holiday Park had their own hot thermal pools. They provided a good soak at the end of the day. We never did make it to the ever-popular Polynesian Spa because we had a similar experience just a few paces from our cabin. In the evenings we also enjoyed a short hike on the property through the bush. Steam wafts up through the undergrowth, giving the eerie feeling of a haunted forest. Just a step off the path I could stand in a hot puddle of mud or a little hot spring of water bubbling up from the ground. At the edge of the lake I would push the sand aside to make a little area to lay in. The small amount of warm water that filled my pool made a perfect hot tub to recline in while watching the sky set ablaze with color as the sun dipped below the horizon.

The major reason to visit Rotorua is to see, smell and feel the crazy things going on inside our earth that are bubbling to the surface there. Located on the Volcanic Plateau, it is one of the most active geothermic fields in the world. Scientists say that the underlying magma chamber of the volcano that is now Lake Rotorua collapsed, creating a circular caldera which filled with water.

On each visit to the city we found ourselves drawn to Kuirau Park, located next to the city center. It was a great place for the kids to run around a bit and get the wiggles out. The number of mud pools and steam vents that you could enjoy in this park for free was amazing! I love free, so my family is used to being dragged to all the free activities over and over again. We wandered around the park, looking into the boiling mud, soaking our feet in the warm footbaths and enjoying the Saturday market.

Ornamental flower gardens filled the park. The steam drifted through the petals to create an enchanted place. The wisteria-laden bridge gave a haunted Monet feeling, while petals from flowering trees carpeted the grass in the spring. Surrounded by this lush beauty, I forgot other areas in nearby parks that are as desolate as the moon because of sulfurous gasses and high ground temperatures. I think it's amazing that the earth can be so radically different in such a small space.

When the kids asked where we were going I simply replied "Hell."

"Where's Hell?" they asked, baffled by my response.

They had no doubt we were in the pit of Hell when we pulled into the parking lot and opened the car door. Assaulted by the smell of sulfur, Elena immediately plugged her nose.

Rotorua's most active geothermal park was named by George Bernard Shaw as he looked across the land and gave it the name "Hellsgate," believing he had indeed arrived at the gates to Hell. Elena tottered down the wooden boardwalks, concentrating on balancing while holding her nose. We came face to face with the raw power of the earth as mud bubbled and boiled around us. Sticky, hot steam floated over the surface of grey pools of water surrounded by dry clay, rocks and barren land. Streams of water flowed through cracks in the mud. We walked up a hill and through an area where trees were able to survive the less-intense heat of the ground. The view of Kakahi Falls, the largest waterfall in the Southern hemisphere, was stunning. The 104°F water made bathing under the falls an enjoyable ritual for Maori warriors. Newborn boys were also baptized under the falls. On the other side, pots of thick mud bubbled and burped, releasing gasses into the air. Spewing mud rather than lava, the only mud volcano in New Zealand is here. The sights around me made me feel as though I had entered the apocalypse. A lonely bird strutted through the water, his long legs delicately feeling their way down the stream. Along the Steaming Cliffs I looked for other signs of life. At the surface of the water the temperature is 250°F. Thick clouds of steam rise to ten feet before dispersing into the air. At the end of the path we walked down to the bank of the Medicinal Sulphur Lake. I scooped up a handful of mud. The grey water streamed through my fingers as I rubbed my hands together. The soft, silky mud dried on my hands, and soothed my skin. Whether on the banks of the Amazon, the shore of the Dead Sea, or in Rotorua, mud is believed by many to have healing powers. For more than seven hundred years the Maori have lived on this site, treasuring it as a place of healing and revitalization. Hellsgate offers spa services and a wide variety of mud products for purchase.

In 1886, earthquakes throughout the North Island were precursors to the violent eruption of Mt. Tarawera. Smoke and ash blasted thousands of meters into the sky. Spewing rock, ash and mud buried the popular tourist village of Te Wairoa. Once considered the eighth wonder of the natural world, the pink and white silica terraces were buried, gone forever. The terraces had formed as water containing silica flowed from the geysers on top of the hill down over lava steps. The water cooled and crystalized, forming giant waterfalls of silica. The elite traveled by ship, steamboat, a coach pulled by horse, and finally by canoe to walk the terraces and sit in the pools of warm water. When the volcano erupted, nearby Lake Rotomahana erupted as well, blowing the picturesque terraces to pieces. This unique geography was lost forever. One hundred fifty people were killed during the eruption as homes filled with ash. Much is still buried today, but as I wandered through the village, I was keenly aware of the level where the earth is not excavated compared to the level prior to the disaster. I hear of disasters in remote places destroying third world villages, but until I actually stood and studied the change in topography, I didn't comprehend the terror an event like this would cause.

A twenty-minute drive south of Rotorua, the Waimangu Volcanic Valley is TripAdvisor's number one rated attraction in Rotorua. Several tours are offered with guides and rides on boats, but we just wanted a day of wandering through the park, to enjoy this unique nature on our own. The same eruption in 1886 that destroyed the silica terraces created the world's youngest geothermal site. Rather than the continual grey and dead feeling in many of the parks, this park has a unique display of color. As we walked along the paths there were so many uncommon sites to see. Emerald pools surrounded by beautiful bushland filled craters with brilliant green water. The green is a result of sphagnum moss which has been used in healing for its extracting properties. Warbrick Terrace is a small fall of water with gold, black, grey and rust colors created by deposits of algae, iron oxide, hydroxide and silicate. Inferno Crater and Frying Pan Lake, the world's largest hot spring, crackled and sizzled as steam floated above them.

It takes perfect planing to arrive in time to see the Lady Knox Geyser erupt at exactly 10:15 a.m. Wai-O-Tapu is another park of volcanic craters, steaming ground and bubbling mud pools. Yet it is unique with its own colors and features. It provides the most diverse and spectacular geothermal area in the Taupo Volcanic Zone. I found the geyser to be intriguing and fun. Unlike America's beauty, Old Faithful, this one needs to be prompted along. In 1901 a gang of prisoners doing laundry discovered that they could make the geyser erupt by adding soap. Every day at 9:45 a.m. a surfactant is poured into the geyser before a crowd of eager onlookers. The soap breaks the surface tension in the cold water chamber causing it to mix with water in the hot chamber. Water and foam begin to bubble over the vent. The fountain grows in speed and height, reaching up to sixty-five feet. The eruption can last as long as an hour, blowing cold water out of the earth. The largest mud pools in the area are constantly bubbling and burping. As bubbles burst, mud is thrown into the air. Champagne Pool hot spring looked like it belonged on another planet. Deep sea-green water looked all the more spooky with steam floating above its surface. It is ringed by a deep orange shoreline created by the mineral antimony. The carbon dioxide that bubbles to the surface gives the large spring its name. Artist's Palette pools show off a rainbow of colors from the various minerals in the mud. Murky green water in Devil's Bath lake comes from the colloidal sulphur and ferrous salts in the ground. Against the white mud rim it gives an eerie appearance.

Because I love learning about the culture of people and places, I visited the Mitai Maori Village several times. It was something I insisted that each of our visitors experience. I do truly believe that if you are only touring New Zealand and don't have the time or opportunity to immerse yourself in Maori culture, make friends and experience the customs first hand, then you need to do some type of dinner and show to gain a bit of insight into this very unique culture. Dinner for the night was a traditional "hangi." The Maori believe the earth is the giver of all life. Just as food grows from soil, it should also be cooked in the ground. A potluck of meats and root vegetables—chicken, lamb and pork with kumara (sweet potato), pumpkin, carrot and potato—were traditionally wrapped in leaves. Today aluminum foil is often used. A pit is dug into the ground, volcanic stones are heated to the white-hot stage with a fire of untreated manuka wood and the food is placed on top of the stones—meat first. The entire hangi is watered to create steam before covering the food with leaves or flax mats and shoveling dirt on top to build the pressure needed to cook the food. The hangi must steam for three hours to be properly cooked. The meal is then lifted from the earth and served. The earth, amount of heat in the rocks, and the type of leaves used all aid to create a unique flavor specific to a traditional hangi. The food is served following an educational walk and cultural show.

The stillness was broken with deep grunts and shouts in Maori that echoed through the dark woods as we walked toward the river. The waka, a traditional canoe, silently slipped into view. Eight warriors chanting in response to their chief paddled in unison. Their bare chests and traditionally tattooed faces and legs presented a threatening show of force. The evening was completed with a form of the haka where their tongues hung out and their eyes bulged from their faces. A shiver ran down my spine as I imagined the fear these warriors invoked in the white man who had never witnessed this before. A guide walked us through the rainforest, pointing out medicinal plants and explaining their traditional uses as we approached the outdoor theater for the nightly performance. We watched the cast in traditional dress explain the history, beliefs and customs of the Maori. They showed us various weapons, beautiful songs and dances using the poi, and games that teach fighting skills. Another fear-inducing haka finished things off. Hungry and with thoughts of the hangi being prepared, we returned to the dining room to enjoy the steaming feast.

Chad is fascinated with the great Redwoods of California. Stories of climbers scaling those great trees, sleeping in their arms and living amongst their branches have been told in our home for years. It's hard to imagine trees so tall and intertwined that they contain completely separate ecosystems in the tops of their branches. Rotorua is the only place outside of the United States where you can wander through a forest of giant California Coastal Redwood trees. Located in the Redwood Memorial Grove surrounding the visitor center, these trees were planted in 1901. Damon claimed that walking through the forest was "like walking through something from a movie, everything was five times as big as normal and you almost expected a T-rex to come hurtling from behind one of the redwood trees." For a boy of twelve, this was a prime spot to let his imagination run wild. Redwoods are amazing plants. A single tree can release up to five hundred gallons of moisture into the air per day. The largest tree in the park is one hundred twenty feet tall, but this is a dwarf in comparison to the nearly three hundred foot trees in California. The kids ran from tree to tree, clasping hands to see if they could reach around the massive trunks. Time will cure this discrepancy as the one hundred ten year old trees of New Zealand continue to grow and age, following in the footsteps of their five hundred year old Californian grandparents.

The seat of a mountain bike is the perfect place to experience the forest trails. Chad is an avid rider and found the park a perfect spot to lose the cares of the world and fly through the forest on a bike. I chose to stay on foot, enjoying the soft paths of needles under my shoes. Beneath the towering redwoods, the iconic ferns of New Zealand create a second world. Ferns seemed to come in every size with colorful names like: umbrella fern, royal fern, European maidenhair, and shining spleenwort. Tree ferns rose above us spreading out like parasols. We waded through fields of knee-high ferns. The silver fern is a medium size tree fern native to New Zealand. As we hunted for these ferns, we identified them by the silver-white color on the underside of the leaves. I marveled at the fern fronds as they began to uncurl. The delicate spiral shape of the silver fern is called the Koru by the Maori. Often seen carved into jewelry and tattooed on bodies, it symbolizes new life, growth, strength and peace. The silver fern symbol—a black background with a white frond—is recognized as a symbol of New Zealand all over the world. First used by the Native Rugby Team in 1888, it has become a part of the national sports teams' emblems, used on military uniforms, and most recently adapted into the New Zealand Coat of Arms.

Queenstown in the South Island is renowned as the adventure capital of the world. Many cities throughout the country offer spectacular opportunities to push the limits. Rotorua has cashed in on the fun, offering a wide assortment of thrilling endeavors. After reading up on a few of the options, we decided to take the children to the Zorb. Basically imagine putting your kids in an oversized hamster ball and pushing them down a hill. Obviously this is fun for the parents as well as the kids. Damon bubbled with excitement as he dove into the center with his sisters following. A bit of warm water sloshed around inside the eleven-foot ball with them. The Zorb is actually a ball within a ball, cushioning the user from harsh bumps along the way. The kids were pushed down the hill. Splashing and rolling around, they tried to sit up while the ball careened down a hill along a winding half-pipe path. From the safety of the sidelines, we heard their screams as they passed. Full of excitement and energy from the thrill, they got in line for another go.

The next great adventure was the luge. I thought of our winter wonderland in Michigan where sleds fly down iced bobsled tracks. I was a bit uncertain how they were going to duplicate this Olympic event in New Zealand. It began with a lovely ride up the mountain in a gondola. The views over the city and lake were breathtaking. The kids trembled with excitement and I had to agree that the ride down the mountain on little carts looked like loads of fun. We raced zooming past one another along the cement path. It was a bit like go-karts powered only by the gravity of the mountain. Over and over again, we went up the gondola then soared down on the luge. New Zealand has it right when they say they know how to do adventure!

The Agrodome claims to be "one of New Zealand's most loved tourist attractions." A "tourist attraction" is definitely the correct term. In a land where there are ten sheep to every person, what better way to spend a day than on a farm? But for the tourist, city slicker, or expat like myself, it is a worthwhile experience. Inside the theater, sheep lined the walls waiting patiently as they posed for many photos. I wasn't prepared for some of the funny-looking sheep with big horns and wrinkly noses. These were sheep that needed a bath. Their thick wool hung heavily on them, ready to be sheared. They each willingly trotted up to their spot on stage during the demonstration. We were told how each breed of sheep benefited New Zealand and what the value of that sheep was. The Merino is the number one best wool sheep, whereas Whiltshires have a tasty meat. The Merino was crossbred with several English breeds to create the Corriedale. Sheep dogs raced onto the stage for a demonstration rounding up ducks. "Hunt away" dogs barked to control the heard and "heading" dogs crouched low to the ground, slowly moving the surrogate sheep in the desired direction. The poor ducks waddled around, finally ending up in a fearful huddle. Kids came on stage for a bottle-feeding contest with greedy little lambs slurping nosily on their food. We finished with a shearing demonstration. The shearer demonstrated lightning quick speed. The clippers zoomed down the skin, leaving piles of wool on the floor. Then he flipped the sheep over and had him sheared before the sheep knew what had hit him. The wool went from the demonstration to the Woollen Mill where we saw the carding, spinning, weaving and knitting processes. All in all, this sheep amusement park was a great way to immerse ourselves in New Zealand's most important industry.

After a long day of touring, a good meal is always welcome. The Pig & Whistle Historic Pub has become one of the most popular bars in Rotorua. Originally built in 1940 as a police station, it is fortified with thick walls of steel covered in brick. Plaster casts of Maori design add a decorative touch to the exterior roofline. An excellent plate of food is the perfect ending to the perfect day.

Rotorua Thermal Holiday Park
Cabins and camping
463 Old Taupo Rd.
Rotorua
www.rotoruathermal.co.nz

Hellsgate
Geothermal park and mud spa
East from Rotorua on SH 30
www.hellsgate.co.nz

Buried Village
1180 Tarawera Rd. RD5
www.buriedvillage.co.nz

Waimangu Volcanic Valley
587 Waimangu Rd. off SH5
www.waimangu.co.nz

Wai-O-Tapu Thermal Wonderland
201 Waiotapu Loop Rd.
www.waiotapu.co.nz

Mitai Maori Village
Our favorite hangi meal and cultural show.
196 Fairy Springs Rd.
www.mitai.co.nz

Tamaki Maori Village
We never visited this village, but it gets excellent reviews.
1220 Hinemaru St.
www.maoriculture.co.nz

The Redwood Forest
Long Mile Rd.
http://www.redwoods.co.nz/

The Zorb
Cnr Western Rd & State Highway 5
www.zorb.com/zorb/rotorua/

The Luge
185 Fairy Springs Rd.

www.skyline.co.nz/rotorua

Agrodome
Western Rd.
www.agrodome.co.nz

Polynesian Spa
Mineral pools and spa therapies
1000 Hinemoa St.
www.polynesianspa.co.nz

Pig & Whistle Historic Pub
1182 Tutanekai Street
www.pigandwhistle.co.nz

<u>River Swim</u>

A bit off the main road between Taupo and Rotorua is a river hidden deep in the woods. Either not many people know about it, or it's so off the beaten path that the word just isn't out. Maybe the adventurous spirit is just lacking in many. Fortunately our visiting friends were in the mood for an adventure.

We followed the directions in our tour book. There were no signs as we wound our way from one road to the next. Eventually we came to a small parking lot where a few camper-vans were parked.

Camper-vans are the most fabulous and intriguing thing in New Zealand. Back home in Michigan I was used to seeing I-75 bumper to bumper with a wide assortment of weekend housing. Cars loaded with the family pulled small pop-up campers, and white haired couples drove $500,000 motorhomes complete with slide-outs and a laundry room. The weekend highways are clogged as everyone makes a mad dash north for refreshment.

Because New Zealand provides opportunity for pure adventure in the wild outdoors, many people take an old truck and create a home for themselves on wheels. Ingenious in their design, they build a cabin of wood on the back of the cab and paint it colorfully. The spirit of a "home away from home" is evident.

It is also possible to rent a van that has been converted into a camper. Many of these have a hippie feel about them. Airbrushing on the outside of fun scenes with graphics or flowers gives this way of traveling a wistful feeling of freedom.

We changed into swimsuits behind a tree then followed a path into the jungle where we chased the sound of running water. The river came into view. A few people sat in different pools along the way. Unlike Morere and other commercialized hot springs, this river is in its natural state.

The water flowed past and tumbled over a small waterfall into a pool before narrowing and continuing on. We stepped out of our shoes and into the water. We found rocks and cubbies to sit in that were warm from natural springs. We played in the water and sat under the falls. Small amounts of steam rose around us, locking us into a fairy world. Little natural surprises like this are what make New Zealand so appealing.

Late in the afternoon we took the road less traveled through Lake Waikeremoana home. The sky lit up as if with fireworks as the sun set over the lake. Soon we were navigating the roads in complete darkness. Little eyes like lights shone out at us in the glow of the headlights.

Small, prickly animals dotted the road. Hedgehogs were brought to New Zealand in the 1870's from Britain. Considered a pest, they eat endangered native giant snails and weta.

Our husbands, the boys, thought it would be great fun to run around in the dark chasing after these little fellows. From the back seat I watched with horror, knowing that with one misstep I would lose my husband forever over the edge of the mountain.

Of course the boys had no fear, so they frolicked and played until we had six hedgehogs secure in the cooler. We created a confined area for them in the laundry room for the night and went to bed. In the morning the kids were thrilled with their new pets. Although not soft and cuddly, they named them, held them, and carried them around.

It is considered a good thing to have a hedgehog living in your garden because they will keep it pest free. I figured I needed every bit of help with my garden enterprise, so we released the little fellows into our Garden of Eden. Sadly, we never saw them again. Although six hedgehogs would have been a bit much romping around our yard, one would have been great fun.

Taupo

A three-hour drive from Wairoa to the center of the North Island brought us to the town of Taupo. Here Lake Taupo, New Zealand's largest lake, discharges into the Waikato River, New Zealand's longest. One of New Zealand's most spectacular waterfalls, Huka Falls, is just a short drive north of town. I enjoyed walking along the Waikato River and across the bridge to get different views of the falls. Jet boats raced up to the falls, giving their passengers a thrilling ride.

Taupo is a place where one can frolic. Water sports such as boating, sailing, swimming, kayaking or parasailing fill days with leisure.

Just north of town I stumbled into a different world at Craters of the Moon Geothermal Walk. The landscape suddenly changed as I entered the park from luscious New Zealand into something out of a sci-fi movie. Steam rose eerily from the earth, the land looked parched and burned. Stubborn, scraggly shrubs that had survived the steam and minerals littered the view. The ground was constantly shifting and changing as steam vents burped and belched sulfuric gasses. A boardwalk wound through the lunar desolation on an otherworldly tour.

The largest geothermal area in New Zealand can be partly credited to human intervention. In the 1950's a power station was built nearby to reduce the pressure of the hot water systems under the surface. Geysers in the valley completely disappeared but the heat output at Craters of the Moon increased, which caused a rise in the hydrothermal eruptions forming the craters. Basically, steam built up under the earth and exploded, causing the deep bowls.

Hukafalls Jet
Jet boat rides to the base of the Huka falls.
http://www.hukafallsjet.com

Craters of the Moon Geothermal Park
http://www.cratersofthemoon.co.nz/html/visitor-s_site.html

Huka Honey Hive
A honey store with a wall made out of an active beehive.
www.hukahoneyhive.com

Life From Death

The little green shoots that sprung from the nutritious soil in my garden grew into healthy, sturdy plants as spring moved to summer. The days grew longer and hotter. I faithfully moved the sprinkler around the garden, caring for my plants as if they were my children.

Stew stopped by often to inspect the plants. Then a few days passed without a visit. I could feel an unusual quiet. The barrier was heavier than just a fence between two yards. I saw him tending his lawn one day and we both wandered over to the fence. I noticed lines etched in his face that weren't there before. The spring was missing from his step. He looked tired.

"Val is in the hospital." he said.

Those few words changed everything. I began to stop by the hospital to visit. The long corridors were as unfamiliar to me as the sickness the walls concealed. A cleaning lady showed me to Val's room. I would sit and chat. Val would fall asleep. Stew would pat my hand and thank me for visiting. An unspoken sadness cried out with cold hands gripping my heart.

One day I saw Stew at the fence. His eyes were vacant and empty. The whites were red with pain. Tears welled up.

"She's gone, Kris."

A tear silently trickled down my cheek. I didn't know how to share the love mixed with grief that was in my heart. I asked when the visiting hours were.

He looked at me strangely and said, "She's at the morgue. Pickering will let you take a look at her if that would make you feel better."

I was shocked. No viewing hours in New Zealand? Just a funeral?

The Maori lay the dead out in their homes. Visitors come for days to weep and mourn with the families before the burial.

The Pakeha, white people, mourn in silence, alone. A few close friends will stop by to drop off a meal and offer condolences. After about three days a funeral is held in the church and the body is buried. It felt so isolated, so alone.

My garden became therapeutic for Stew. He would often stop by with a spade.

"We can't let those weeds grow, Kris." he would say before tromping with a heavy soul into the backyard to work in the dirt a bit. The small little seedlings, watered with tears, grew into full size plants producing an abundance of fresh food.

As my garden grew I began harvesting its bounty. I gathered new recipes to prepare from the abundance of produce I had. I shared many meals with Stew so that he could enjoy the harvest as well.

A few things had popped up in my garden that I did not plant. "Pumpkins." Stew said. He showed me how to make a mound with a moat around it. Three plants per mound. The pumpkins took off, shooting out into the yard and all over my garden. I learned that the thick, black, volcanic soil of New Zealand will grow anything

The pumpkins were a very typical New Zealand variety. Not the common bright orange Halloween pumpkin we know in the States, these have grey skin and are excellent for cooking. Each of my little plants gave me about five pumpkins. From each pumpkin I got two pies, two batches of muffins, and a pot of soup. We ate pumpkin cooked with a roast, pumpkin as a side dish, pumpkin in soup. I groaned each time I visited a friend and they happily handed me a pumpkin from their garden. Little did they know I had a growing stack in my backyard!

Stew and I had walked through the valley of the shadow of death together. Because of a little backyard plot of earth, he found life through a garden and I found life in a friendship.

Pumpkin Muffins
From April Daum

2 cups flour
2 tsp. baking powder
¼ tsp. baking soda
1 tsp. ground cinnamon
¾ tsp. ground ginger
1/8 tsp. ground allspice
1/8 tsp. ground cloves
½ tsp. salt
½ cup butter, melted & cooled
¾ cup packed light brown sugar
¾ cup pure pumpkin (canned or cooked)
¼ cup well-shaken buttermilk
2 large eggs
1 tsp. vanilla extract
3 Tbs. raw green pumpkin seeds (hulled)

1. Preheat oven to 400°F. Butter pan or use cupcake papers.
2. Stir flour, baking powder, baking soda, spices and salt in large bowl.
3. In separate bowl, cream butter, brown sugar, pumpkin, buttermilk, eggs and vanilla. Add to dry ingredients and stir until just combined, then stir in Pumpkin seeds. (3 Tbs. Raisins optional as well.)
4. Divide batter among 12 muffin cups.
5. Make crumble topping: ½ cup flour; ½ cup brown sugar, 2 Tbs. soft butter—cut in until crumbly. Spoon on muffins before baking.
6. Bake 20 min.

Earthquakes

    A 25,000 mile horseshoe in the Pacific Ocean comprises an area called the Ring of Fire. Although there is a bit of a romantic heat to the title, this deadly ring boasts four hundred fifty two volcanoes and ninety percent of the world's earthquakes. Large plates of earth collide and slide under each other, releasing a tremendous amount of energy. Melting rock rises to the surface as lava pushes through and erupts in a volcano.

The arc stretches from New Zealand, around the eastern edge of Asia, north across Alaska and south along the coasts of North and South America.

It seems that more and more frequently as we sit in our living rooms in front of the TV, we see reports of volcanoes, earthquakes and tsunamis as they wreak their destruction on our earth.

Previously, I had only lived north of this ring so I observed earthquakes from the safe distance of the news. The whole thought of the earth rumbling, the house shaking, things falling off shelves and breaking seemed terrifying to me.

The western end of the ring ran straight through New Zealand, which set me a bit on edge. I felt like I was walking on pins and needles, wondering if the house would fall down around me or a great surge of water would come rushing up the river, pulling us all to our death at any moment. Every hotel, school and public building had signs posted with "What to do in the event of a volcano or earthquake." These signs seemed a bit more threatening than the ones I was used to in Michigan showing fire escape routes and "What to do in case of a tornado."

It is estimated that 20,000 earthquakes occur in New Zealand every year. According to my math, that's fifty-five a day. Yikes! Only about two hundred of these are strong enough to be felt, but still, the odds were that I was going to have to learn how to deal with it.

Despite the fact that most of the earthquakes are just little shakes, New Zealanders live with the reality that disaster is always a possibility. Folks in Wairoa told me about the eruptions of Mt. Ruapehu, the most active volcano in New Zealand, in 1995 and 1996. They spoke of airports being closed, water outages and the general annoyance of cleaning up the ash that fell on the town.

More recently was the February 2011 earthquake that devastated Christchurch in the South Island. This 6.3 magnitude quake hit the second-largest city in the middle of the day, causing significant damage to the central Canterbury region and killing one-hundred-eighty-five people.

One morning, a month into our adventure, Chad claimed that I had experienced my first earthquake.

"Huh?" I said.

"Don't you remember waking me and asking me to stop shaking the bed?"

"Huh?"

"I said I wasn't shaking the bed, but you insisted that I was."

"Huh?"

"Then I heard Damon's bed hitting the wall. You don't remember this?"

"Huh?"

I looked around the room trying to make sense of what he was saying. Everything was in place. Makeup bottles were still standing— maybe things had shifted but I couldn't tell. I declared that there was no way an earthquake could have happened, because everything was fine! Chad began to doubt himself and commented, "Maybe I was having a dream."

In the kitchen, my Sigg bottle was upside down draining. Triumphantly I pronounced, "There is no way we had an earthquake because this bottle would have tipped over very easily." I gave the bottle a little flick and tossed my hair over my shoulder just to make my point.

We turned on the news just to see if Chad was dreaming. Indeed, at 11:25 p.m. a 5.9 quake had struck ten kilometers southwest of Hastings at a depth of thirty kilometers. The shake lasted about twenty seconds and an aftershock of 3.0 was felt a bit later.

So what did that mean to us there in Wairoa? From what I heard around town, "It was a good one." The shake woke people up and made them wonder if there was more to come. The depth and distance softened the quake. I felt a bit cheated that I didn't actually wake up and remember being rattled a bit as everyone else in town seemed to.

Over the year, members of my family felt several earthquakes. I always seemed to be sleeping, driving the car, or leaping through the air and missed the shake. A few were even noteworthy enough to make the newspaper.

So although I never noticed an earthquake, tremor or slight shifting of any sort, the reality of disaster striking at any moment was not one to be toyed with. Take a moment to read the "what to do in the event of..." signs in your hotel. Better to be safe than to be sorry.

The Dump

It may seem like an odd thing to write about, but the dump was a part of my normal routine in Wairoa. Garbage, or rather rubbish, removal came once a week. Like most civilized places, you bought your garbage bags, filled them up, then put them by the curb to be taken away. But this turned out to be a very costly way to get rid of my trash, so like many people in town I began taking it directly to the dump.

A short drive out of town, the dump proved to be a very interesting place. I expected chaos but found order. As I drove up the long driveway, I saw a large pile of scrap metal like old gutted cars and appliances. Further up the drive the recycle center greeted me with places for brown and green glass, clear glass, milk jugs, clear food plastic, cleaning containers, paper, cardboard and of course numbers one and two plastics. This place was actually making me happy! I love order and here they had a place for everything. Never mind the growing smell as I drove closer to the actual garbage pit or the birds that circled overhead.

Further down the road I came to a hut next to a large scale in the road. How cool was that? I drove onto the scale and waited while the car rocked back and forth a bit then the man in the hut waved me on saying I could "toss my rubbish over the wall."

So I drove up to the wall, got out of the car, was hit by a wave of stink, and looked over the edge. Sure enough, about six feet down was a freshly plowed area to throw my trash. I looked to my left and saw a field of everyone else's debris. Yuck. I ran to the trunk of my car and threw my trash over the edge as fast as I could. I quickly learned to back the car up to the wall, suck in a deep breath of car-fresh air then run quickly to the trunk and fling my garbage to the wind. All this while dodging white bombs falling from the birds circling overhead. Some things are the same no matter where you go.

I jumped into my car and drove back to the hut and onto the scale. Amazing! With a slight sway that big scale could recognize that I left fifteen pounds of garbage behind. The man in the hut said, "$1.30 for your load of rubbish."

As I drove away I began to ponder how efficient and inexpensive this system was. In striking contrast to keeping a large trash can in my garage and filling it to the point of overflowing each week, this encouraged people to recycle. A quick look over the edge into the pit forces one to consider what is happening to our environment.

The wilderness areas of the world are precious gems that we are losing as the population of the world grows and our demands to consume products increases. Some may wonder why we should be concerned with the environment. Past generations acted on a lack of knowledge and today we are dealing with the consequences.

As we look to the future we need to decide what type of world we wish to leave to generations after us.

It's easy to expect others to take this responsibility for us, but the government can't fix all the problems in society. It's up to individuals to claim responsibility and make changes. Experiencing the dump in New Zealand touched off a journey for me to examine and change my personal habits in light of the greater need of the environment.

The first step in change is to realize the *need* for change. There is so much in our daily lives that we don't take the time to seriously think about.

What will happen to this article after I am done using it?

What is left in the air after a drive to town?

How is heating my house affecting the air that I breathe?

How many years until this dump is full and then where does the rubbish go?

Is there a way I can reduce the amount that I am contributing to this each week?

The mantra "Reduce, Reuse, Recycle" began haunting my dreams as I looked for ways to improve my care of the earth.

New Zealand is miles ahead of America in the average person's care of the environment. I reduced my waste to one small bag a week with my recycling container overflowing. I found that most packaging contains the recycling symbol, yet there was still room for improvement.

New Zealanders currently recycle seventy percent of their aluminum, fifty percent of their paper, forty five percent of their glass, thirty percent of their steel and only eighteen percent of their plastics.

Composting was our next goal. A friend showed me how to compost with bins and worm farms. Most people in Wairoa composted—compared to the one person I knew in America who did. The town council even came up with a compost system that also helped produce a liquid fertilizer for your garden. Soon I found that all my vegetation scraps were magically being transformed into fertile soil for my flowers.

Conscious living can also be fun and rewarding. At a party we went to the host had one hundred percent edible—thus compostable—plates and wooden eating utensils. Everyone had fun standing in line munching on their dinnerware! Every plate had a bite taken out of it even before food was piled on.

My kids often did projects at school employing the concept of reusing something old to create something new. I even had a friend who made his own bio-diesel fuel for his car by recycling vegetable oil.

On a greater scale, I discovered that businesses who display the black square with the white fern have achieved the Qualmark. This is New Zealand's official mark of quality for tourism. Businesses are assessed on their environmental performance in areas of energy efficiency, conservation initiatives, waste management, community activities and water conservation.

As we traveled I saw these principles practiced daily in garbage separation and composting in hotels, light switches that were activated with room entrance keys, energy efficient light bulbs and recycling containers at camping grounds.

You don't need to carry a picket sign in a demonstration march or wear a t-shirt proclaiming 'Save the Whales' to care about the future of the earth. Each person has the power to make a difference. I urge you to stop, think, consider and evaluate. Small choices each of us make on a daily basis will change the world. We will leave a gift to future generations through all of us making conscious decisions.

Napier

I studied design in college. Long nights were spent pouring hours into learning the intricacies of each architectural style and the nuances and transitions to the next style. That's why I was extremely excited to visit Napier long before we landed in New Zealand. It was one of those mandatory places on my list "to visit, explore and become intimate with." To the south, Napier was the other option for a day in the city. The one and a half hour drive was hilly and windy so I always made sure ginger cookies were stowed in my purse. We had our traditional pull-over spot along the way to give everyone a breather and to allow stomachs to settle before we continued the journey.

I fell in love with this city from the moment I first saw it. The ocean, parks and water bring vibrant life to the city. There is a downtown shopping district with restaurants, cafes, shops and a bookstore. But for me the main attraction was the Art Deco architecture predominant throughout the town.

On February 3, 1931, Napier was struck by the largest earthquake to ever hit New Zealand. Very few buildings survived the 7.8 magnitude quake and subsequent fires. Over one hundred people were killed.

In a rush to rebuild, architectural students were called in from Auckland. Art Deco was at its height so Napier went mad for the bold, geometric style. Napier is now considered one of the finest concentrated collections of Art Deco in the world. Who would have guessed that I would have found such a treasure in a tiny town on the east coast of New Zealand?

The Art Deco period ran from 1925-1939. "Style Moderne" was the original name, but following the 1925 Exposition of Decorative Arts in Paris, people began using the term "Art Deco." It is purely a decorative style based on mathematical and geometric shapes with influences from Africa, Egypt, Mexico and the Machine Age. Art Deco's broad influence touched such varied pursuits as architecture, interior design, art, film and fashion. Steam liners and skyscrapers were in the beginnings of their existence at this time. Bold steps and sweeping curves give a dramatic line to the overall style, with the sunburst motif the most iconic of the era. Stainless steel, inlaid wood, and zebra skins provide dramatic contrast in texture and color. Art Deco was an opulent style in reaction to the austerity of World War I. Cut short by World War II, it opened the door for Modernism.

A stroll down the streets of Napier made me feel as though I had stepped back to a time when cars were new on the scene. The buildings, lampposts, sewer covers, fountains and other little details all spoke of a time of renewal following disaster for this town.

Every third weekend in February, Napier celebrates their unique architecture with a festival. One of the first events to kick off the weekend is a trip on an antique steam train from Napier to Wairoa.

It was a beautiful day and the kids were in school. Chad rang up to tell me the steam train would be coming to town. I met him at lunchtime and we went down to the old train platform to watch it arrive. I was surprised at first to see the area abuzz with stalls selling strawberry shortcakes, honey, sausages and tea sandwiches, but then I realized our little town doesn't see this much excitement very often.

We heard a cry of "Here she comes!" The sound of the whistle blasting vibrated through the air before we could see the train. I felt excitement pulse around me and believed I had stepped back into another time. As the train pulled up, women with furs and hats, and men with suspenders leaned out of the windows and waved to us. We watched as they disembarked, so nostalgic-looking with gloves on their hands and canes in tow. Dressed to the hilt in Art Deco style, some even had wicker picnic baskets packed with lunch to enjoy under a tree. We mingled, enjoying the atmosphere, then went to take a look at the train.

My Grandfather used to work on a steam engine so I found it especially fascinating to watch the engineers check gauges and oil gears. Coal was shoveled into a fiery, hissing furnace. It took a full hour to be sure everything was in proper order before they could turn the engine around to head back.

The conductor came around yelling "all aboard," encouraging passengers to re-embark for their return journey to Napier. The train began to hiss and chug as it gained speed, and the wheels clacked on the tracks. People waved goodbye out the windows as the red caboose disappeared in the distance. Just as the smoke dissolved into the sky, so did my jaunt into the past fade away. Yet, the weekend was just beginning.

I ran into a friend and she grabbed my arm saying she was headed downtown to some second-hand stores to outfit herself for their day in Napier. I went along and together we found some hats and gloves to add to clothes we'd found in our closets to complete our Art Deco attire.

Saturday morning, the girls and I got dressed in high 30's fashion. My two little girls sat on the floor with straw hats on their heads, carefully dressing their American Girl Dolls in special outfits for the event. Soon the family was ready to go. I was in a sort of dreamlike state during this particular ride to the city.

Our first stop was the old Tobacco Co. building where we had a tour of the interior. This excellent sample of Art Deco with flairs of Art Nouveau showcased adornments of roses, raupo and grapevines around the elegantly curved entrance. From there we headed downtown where we spent the rest of the day. We took our time walking around, soaking in the atmosphere. Many people had thrown themselves into the spirit of things by dressing to the style of the era. There was a women's choral group singing old war songs, a jazz street group and an organ grinder complete with a monkey. People strolled along. Some stopped to listen while others found seats to enjoy the spectacle.

We meandered along and found a good corner to view the upcoming auto parade. Over two hundred antique cars rolled past, shined to perfection. I was told that twelve shipping containers arrive from America each year with cars for the parade. The New Zealand Navy marched past as they do each year in commemoration of the Navy's response and aid during the 1930's disaster. Of course no auto show would be complete without a rebel bike group to stir things up!

After the auto parade it was time to lay back and relax a bit. A glass of freshly squeezed lemonade hit the spot. Chad and the kids found a patch of grass under a tree to read a book. There was a tent set up with women getting their hair done in high fashion for evening dancing and dinners.

I wandered over to the band shelter where a time era Costumes & Coiffure fashion competition was in progress. As I sat on the grass, I enjoyed the band's lively dance tunes in the background. People were swing dancing in the audience while women strutted their stuff on stage. I leaned back with one eye on the ocean, and the other on the stage. The music was playing, and a breeze was on my face. Out of nowhere a WWII plane came swooping down. What a show it made zig zagging across the sky! I was sad to see this day come to an end, but like all good things, it must. I am glad I was able to stop for a moment and step back in time to experience days gone by.

Beyond the enchantment of the Art Deco architecture, Napier has much to offer. It was easy to spend a day wandering Marine Parade, visiting boutiques, enjoying a coffee and having a true Italian Pizza before heading home.

Another part of the city we enjoyed was the Ahuriri neighborhood. Only a five-minute drive from the city center, this area along the harbor was a fabulous mix of traditional fisherman's cottages, new apartments and industrial warehouses. A trendy, reborn feeling brought life to the area. A stroll along the boardwalk in the evening before dining at one of the many restaurants was enjoyable. This area will suit all tastes from bars to fine dining.

Because this is New Zealand and there are sheep on every hill, in the yards and even grazing amongst the grape vines, a tour through a sheepskin factory seemed like the thing to do. Napier has an excellent one. At first glance while driving by I thought I was looking at laundry drying in the wind, but upon closer inspection I realized that hundreds of sheepskins had been hung to dry as part of the cleaning process.

The factory buys large quantities of skins from ranchers to make into products to export, but individuals can bring in skins from their sheep to have them cleaned as well. This is exactly what we did with the skins from our two pet sheep.

The skins were marked, then put in large vats to wash all the grossness from the fur. A hillside of sheep grazing and dotting the pastures is quite picturesque, but upon closer inspection I realized that the white wool had sticks in it. Legs and tummies were muddy from tramping around all day then laying in the dirt to rest. And I didn't even want to think of their backside and what was caked in there. So a bath for the skins is a must. The huge vats for washing have large agitators to stir the skins up and get rid of all the debris. It takes three days to get the skins clean and tanned before they can be dried. We all know how our favorite wool sweaters shrink right up to doll size when put in the drier, so the skins are laid on a mesh surface, stretched and clipped in place before the dryers are turned on. After six hours the next process is to iron and polish and fluff them up with a big roller. Six weeks later it was time to pick up my skins. All fresh and white, they were ready to be thrown on my couch, a great reminder of the little guys that used to frolic in our backyard. The extra skins were graded by size, cut into pieces and made into anything that could be dreamed up.

The shop was a lot of fun with everything from sheepskin steering wheel covers to slippers and skins for your bed.

Children need a reward from time to time—we all do. But I had observed my kids at home and felt that they were complete barbarians in their table manners. I don't think of myself as a prissy, but I also don't think of myself as uncultured. Picking up vegetables with their fingers, not using a napkin, slurping milk—all of these habits grated on my nerves and I dreaded the thought of their first date and the horror it would bring to their companion.

We decided to do something to correct the long list of faults and felt a reward would be necessary to accomplish this. It couldn't be an ordinary reward, a trip to the ice cream store or such, rather it had to be one worthy of the work needed to right the wrongs.

The prize was to be dinner at a fancy restaurant. We believed the kids could attain the standard necessary to join in fine dining without me, their mom, having to cringe in discomfort at childish manners. I do believe it is possible to rear children who are not screaming at the table or running around the restaurant like banshees.

We set our eyes on a special meal at the Old Church restaurant in Napier and began our research of what proper table manners are. Using the Internet, the kids came up with a list of habits that were absent in our household and began to work on them.

Like magic they began to notice when someone was talking with food in their mouth—something that I was often guilty of—when the napkin was by the plate rather than on a lap, or when too large of a bite was taken, puffing their cheeks like little chipmunks. We began the practice of passing all food in one direction around the table and placing our silverware on our plate at ten o'clock to four o'clock when we were done eating.

Our goal was to go two weeks without a member catching another one in a mistake. Honestly, this was not an easy goal. I had as many bad habits to reform as the children did. Propping my elbows on the table was a hard habit to break. After about five months we reached our goal.

On the big day we headed early to Napier, arrived without incident, and everyone's stomach felt well. We found a boutique hair salon and the females in the family were treated to much needed hairdo's. A lovely day gave us the getaway that all families need from time to time. Late in the afternoon we changed into the nicest clothes we owned. The girls looked lovely in their skirts and blouses and Damon dapper in a sweater and slacks.

As the sun sank low on the horizon, we pulled up the long tree-lined drive sparkling with magical white lights. I heard a breath of awe come from the back seat. The white church greeted us with light pouring from stained glass windows. More lights twinkled on the grapevines surrounding the church.

The enchanting church coupled with the children's anticipation created an atmosphere of mystical delight amongst our family. We quietly entered the lobby that sparkled with glass ornamentation and gilded decorations. Seated by an open doorway, I could hear the fountain in the courtyard gurgling its pleasure. A mixture of colonial architecture with chic decoration created a nostalgic atmosphere. Crystal chandeliers, velvet chairs, wood floors and airy curtains spoke of refinement and class. Jazz from a string trio floated in the air.

Giggles arrived with Shirley Temples and virgin daiquiris. Each person picked the most succulent sounding entree off the menu. Every proper table manner was followed with precision. The kids sat straight and tall with napkins smoothed on their laps and hands folded while they waited in anticipation. Dessert brought another round of smiles as white plates adorned with syrupy squiggles bore delicacies garnished with spun sugar. Fit for angels, my cherubs delicately ate their treats.

I noticed sleepy heads bobbing in the back while I gazed contentedly out the window during the drive home through the mountains. The wonder of the evening lay warming me like a cloak on my shoulders.

GEON Art Deco Weekend
www.artdeconapier.com

National Aquarium of New Zealand
Marine Parade, Napier
www.nationalaquarium.co.nz

Classic Sheepskins
22 Thames Street
Pandora, Napier
www.classicsheepskins.co.nz

The Silky Oak Chocolate Company & Chocolate Museum
1131 Links Rd.
Napier
www.silkyoakchocs.co.nz

The Old Church Restaurant and Bar
199 Meeanee Road
Napier
www.theoldchurch.co.nz

http://www.mannersinternational.com/etiquette_tips_table.asp

Wine

New Zealand was my introduction to the world of wine. Wine was something that I simply had not thought about up to that point. Snooty wine clubs in the U.S. turned me off from the whole culture of wine.

But in New Zealand wine is like water. In fact, they don't seem to have something to drink with a meal unless it is a glass of wine. I went through so many dinners parched because there wasn't a glass for me to drink water from. It was baffling.

As my experience widened I felt that I needed to be able to hold a glass of wine in my hand and have some knowledge of what I could choke down, what was completely detestable, and what I actually enjoyed. I know this seems completely unfathomable to many people, but it is simply the culture I had lived in up to that point. I was finding that my preconceived notions were slowly changing.

For a country as tiny as New Zealand, they are making an amazing splash on the worldwide wine industry. In 2009 they were ranked the fourteenth country in wine production. I can stroll my local grocery store in Michigan and find a New Zealand wine section. The Marlborough region is the largest producer, with Hawke's Bay the second. A drive down the bay took me through vineyards and past wineries. I certainly needed to understand more!

New Zealand vineyards are very picturesque. Sheep wander and graze amongst grape-laden vines. One day I asked my husband to pull into the driveway of a vineyard so that I could take a few pictures. It was a sort of snap decision, so he did a last minute on-two-wheels turn into the driveway. We rolled in and then… *thunk.* We had hit the flagpole at the end of the long driveway up to the winery. Even sitting inside the car we could clearly see that the pole no longer stood tall and proud, but rather looked limp as it bent towards the ground.

Slowly we got out, walked around the pole and contemplated our options. We decided that the first task was to try and right our wrongs. We had the kids get out of the car. We were on a country type road where a vehicle passed about every sixty seconds. The littlest kid stood watch. As soon as the road was clear, on Chad's command the rest of us would push with all our might on the pole. As soon as Elena, shouted we would stop, put our hands in our pockets, look around and try to appear completely innocent. After the car sped past we would go back to our pushing.

After awhile we realized we weren't going to be able to straighten the pole, so with our shoulders sagging in defeat we piled back into the car and slowly drove up the endlessly long driveway. Because we were heading home after a long weekend in Wellington, we were a bit on the rugged-looking side of things. We walked into the spotless boutique showroom. A woman greeted us. Immediately assuming that we were there to sample their wines she began to educate us on the intricacies of their processes. Chad was hooked, but eventually he was able to get a word in and explained our pole-hitting accident.

The owner was away for the weekend so she sent the viticulturist (who was an American with a bachelors in wine making) to survey the damage. We were now stuck in the fancy showroom with the sommelier. More fancy words were thrown around as we sipped various samples of wine. I felt very uneducated in the wine world. When she stepped out for a moment, Chad and I had a hurried conversation, agreeing that neither of us cared for any of the wines that we had tasted yet we felt highly obligated to purchase a bottle because their flag pole was now crooked.

The viticulturist returned saying "No worries." He had used the tractor to right the pole. Leaving with our over-priced bottle of undrinkable wine, I shot a few sorry pictures as we drove down the long driveway and returned home.

The maritime climate of New Zealand is ideal for wine growers. The two main characteristics are precipitation and prevailing winds. Sometimes we would go through weeks of consistent, intense wind and I would begin to hear the old stories of people who had gone crazy due to the wind. The warm—but not hot—summer, and cool—but not cold—winters are also a necessary climate for good wine. I got a sense of how important this was when spring had a few unexpected frosts. Russell was called night after night to fly his helicopter low over the vineyards to prevent the frost from destroying the crops during the critical hours before the sun rose to warm the air. The expense of hiring a helicopter was offset by the profit expected from a good year of wine.

Our final wine experience was a trip to Napier and the Hawke's Bay region with friends we collected over the year. The New Zealand wine industry actually began in Hawke's Bay at Mission Estate. A group of French Missionaries arrived in 1838 and established a mission. Vines were planted to produce table wine and sacramental wine. The eight hundred acre estate was eventually sold. The site became the community parish and the new mission site became a seminary and the center of winemaking activities. As wine production grew, buildings were added to the property. Today Mission Estate has a well-respected reputation for consistent quality and value for your money. The estate is vast. The cellar is located in a restored seminary building.

Church Road, a boutique winery, presented us with the best overall education on the wine making process. Huge oak vats holding unfathomable amounts of wine filled a room. Our guide explained the process in detail. In the underground cellar we saw the original storage and barrels which are still used. The first commercial Cabernet Sauvignon was produced here in 1949 by Tom McDonald. Following the tour we were able to sample a variety of wines.

The various ways showrooms choose to present their wine tastings adds to the fun. In some, we walked around the showroom, stopping to sample different wines along the way. In others, we sat at a table in the restaurant as they presented each sample in a more formal fashion.

We finished the evening with dinner at Elephant Hill Winery. As the sun set, the Pacific Ocean reflected the brilliant hues of red, orange and yellow. We settled deep into our seats at the relatively new, chic restaurant to enjoy the fine menu before the drive home. It was the perfect ending to a perfect day.

The alluvial valleys of New Zealand provide excellent soil drainage. The ground is rocky and loose. Wineries had vases of dirt and rocks sitting next to various bottles of wine to showcase the soil that grapes were grown in to produce a specific wine. In fact, Gimblett Gravels is the riverbed that was left behind when the Ngaruroro River changed direction following the flood of 1867. The land is high in gravel and low in fertility, making it impossible to graze sheep. In a land of agriculture, it appeared good for nothing. Then in 1981 a few pioneer wine growers came in and began producing some of the world's finest full bodied red wines. The wines produced in this soil are so remarkable that "Gimblett Gravels" is often mentioned on the wine label.

The majority of growers in New Zealand are small boutique vineyards producing niche varieties. Think "family owned" and you will understand the care that goes into each bottle of wine. Viticulturists choose very small sections of the vineyard for each grape. Each year they carefully inspect the grapes selecting certain vines to age in special barrels for a specific amount of time. The results are remarkable. We are not talking about operations that mass-produce their product, throwing in grapes from all over the country. This is a glass of wine where life slows down for awhile. You appreciate the graceful flow as you swirl your glass and breathe in the aroma before you take a sip. The flavor lingers on your tongue just as the experience lingers in your mind. Wine is no longer something that is casually thrown in the cart at the grocery store, but has become as much an art to drink as it was to produce.

Church Road Winery & Museum
150 Church Road
Taradale, Hawke's Bay
www.churchroad.co.nz

Mission Estate Winery
198 Church Road
Poraiti, Napier
http://www.missionestate.co.nz

Elephant Hill Winery
86 Clifton Road
Te Awanga, Hawke's Bay
www.elephanthill.co.nz

American Culture Collides

One of the reasons I like to venture out into the world is that I want to experience something different. Life at home begins to feel blasé and I get the itch to throw my system into shock for a while and leave all familiarity behind.

The interesting thing about being an American is that it is becoming more and more difficult to do this. I travel into the thick of the Amazon and floating in the water next to my boat is a plastic bottle with English words on the label. I venture deep into the heart of Africa and Disney videos are playing on the TV in a one room hut. New Zealand proved to be no different.

I stood in line at the gas station waiting for the "ladies." Evanescence played overhead. I took a glance at the magazine rack and realized I wouldn't lose any sleep wondering how Brad and Angie were doing or if Lindsey was going to make it through another round of rehab. We walked across the street where a window of flashing TV's caught my attention. I paused as George Clooney spoke to a talk show host—and thus the world—about his latest flick.

American pop culture is shaping the world. This could be seen as a good thing or maybe you're like me and you feel a sadness creeping in at the realization that the world bases its perception of America on what it sees coming from Hollywood. Marriages are dysfunctional and housewives hate one another. Of course we all live in mansions, have maids and drive slick sports cars. We can't speak a sentence without cursing God and everyone around us while sleeping with whomever suits us at whatever moment we are so inclined. There are no consequences for our actions because indeed, we are Americans.

This is not the truth of my life. I love the life I've lived in America. I have had the best neighbors who have watched out for me, loved me and grown to be close friends. My house and car and kids are very average. Our kids love being on sports teams in the community where we have grown to know many people.

As I travel and soak in living abroad, I want to leave an impression of America that is appealing in its own adventurous way. America has created things that are great and can benefit society, but other societies often have aspects that can benefit the average American.

Waitomo Caves

Music of the Night
by Andrew Lloyd Webber

Night time sharpens, heightens each sensation
Darkness wakes and stirs imagination
Silently the senses abandon their defenses
Helpless to resist the notes I write...
For I compose the music of the night

Slowly, gently, night unfurls its splendor
Grasp it, sense it, tremulous and tender
Hearing is believing, music is deceiving

Hard as lightening, soft as candlelight.
Dare you trust the music of the night?

Close your Eyes –
For your eyes will only tell the truth
And the truth isn't what you want to see
In the dark it is easy to pretend
That the truth is what it ought to be.

Close your eyes –
Start a journey through a strange new world
Leave all thoughts of the world you knew before[5]

I floated down the river on water of glass broken only by the movement of the boat. Not a sound was in the air, the silence making a song of its own in this magical place. The darkness was as thick as ink in a pot. Millions of tiny star-like lights twinkled like diamonds hanging from the roof above. This place was enchanted.

Glowworms are a bioluminescent insect found in damp caves and overhanging banks in the bush at night in New Zealand and Australia. The most famous place to experience their illusion is at Waitomo Caves. In the dark, all that can be seen is a tiny light beckoning and welcoming the curious visitor—and that is exactly what this insect wishes to do. The larva weaves a nest out of silk then spins up to seventy silver threads hanging down around its nest. Drops of mucus dot the threads. The derrière of the larva glows to attract its prey, who gets caught in the threads of silk. After the larva goes into the pupa stage, it emerges as an adult. The adult uses its sexy light to attract a mate. Adults have no way to eat so they only live a few days.

The adventure begins before setting foot inside the caves. The night before our tour, we took a hike on the trails around the caves located at our campgrounds. Tiny lights began twinkling as the night turned dark. Well equipped with torches (flashlights), we made our way down the trail, hunting for these little lights. Sparkles of light peeked out though little cracks and holes in the rock wall along the path. Although we didn't find many, it whetted our appetite for the next day.

There are many ways to experience the caves around Waitomo. Traditional tours begin by walking through one of the caves. Lighted paths guide the way through the much-traveled caverns. The guide points out the many geological features such as stalagmites, stalactites and cave coral, all beautiful treasures hidden deep within the earth. The lights are turned out for a few moments so that the group can experience the darkness, but you know twenty other people are right there—you are not alone.

In a cave I am aware of the cool, damp air. I can smell that I am deep under the surface of the earth. All is quiet except for the sound of water echoing as it drips. The river running through the cave is unique to the Waitomo Glow Worm Cave. Deep inside, we descended some steps and proceeded into a boat. We floated silently down the river, afraid to break the magical moment. This experience is quiet, easy and serene.

In contrast is the option to go "black water rafting" through the cave. We've all heard of and may have even gone "white water rafting." The "white water" comes from the bubbling rapids that shoot your boat along. It's great fun to fly down a river in a raft, paddling like crazy to keep from turning over. "Black water rafting" is nothing like this. Rather than being together in a raft, each person is given his own personal tire tube. I put on a clammy, musty-smelling wet suit and helmet then tramped off into the woods, following my guide to a hole in the ground. I crawled into the cave, dragging my tube with me, walked a bit, then came to a three foot drop-off to the river below. The only lights were the ones on my group's helmets. The river flowing deep inside the cave was black with no light to show depth or color. I bent over, squeezed my butt into the tube, then fell bottom first into the river below. I hit the water, went under, then popped back up. Complete and utter darkness surrounded me and I felt a chill creeping deep inside. Alone. I began mental exercise. I had to focus on the thought that there was a way out of this cave. This experience wasn't about seeing the cool formations of rock, but about the gripping reality of leaving the lighted world behind and spending some time in darkness. Slowly I began to feel one with the cave. I was not merely observing this cave in my neat, tidy clothes, warm and dry, but rather blinded, cold and wet. I stumbled over rocks, felt the wall to guide me, waded through the river, jumped in and then paddled the tube with my hands. Every fiber of my being could feel the cold of the water and the solitude of the cave. I relied on my headlamp, the sound of a voice or the touch of a person to remind me that I was not alone. When I was able to relax a bit I looked up and was in awe of the host of glowworms speckling the ceiling. I lay back, imagining I was staring into the black night with little stars from heaven twinkling down. Finally light gleamed from a mossy hole in the distance. I walked forward through the black water and found solid footing on the moss-covered rocks disguising the entrance. I climbed back into the world of the living. With my tube tucked under my arm I felt like an original explorer of the cave.

Waitomo Top 10 Holiday Park
12 Waitomo Caves Rd.

Waitomo Caves
www.waitomopark.co.nz

Waitomo Tours
www.waitomo.com

<u>Wellington</u>

Wellington is a city of museums, gardens, culture and dining and it was our favorite urban area to visit in New Zealand. The stunning harbor is located at the south end of the North Island. It is said that Wellington has more cafes, bars and restaurants per capita than New York City. A perfect day for us would begin by rolling out of bed and enjoying a mochaccino and French pastry at one of the cafes on Cuba Street. I had no problem quenching my thirst for coffee in this city where Voyeur Magazine wrote that Wellington was "…fast becoming better known for its long blacks rather than its All Blacks."

I loved the hours of wandering the streets in the Cuba Quarter. This historic area was named after an 1840 settler ship. Eclectic shopping and trendy restaurants line the streets. Vintage clothing stores possess treasures to be discovered. The bohemian feel lends an air of creativity and mystery. From nationally acclaimed restaurants to graffiti-filled alleyways, visitors and locals alike find something of interest along its streets. I fit right in strolling along with my newly purchased ukulele under one arm and a coffee in my hand.

In my opinion the best thing to see in Wellington is the national Te Papa Museum. It's free—need I say more? The freeness meant that with kids in tow we could pop in, spend a few hours and return the next time we were in town to see some more. I never had that guilty feeling of not getting my money's worth! The relaxed pace we were able to take allowed us to visit every nook and cranny of the museum. Hands-on activities such as the life size, hand-carved marae or a good shake in the Earthquake House kept all of us engaged each visit. The world's largest specimen of a colossal squid is a disgustingly curious exhibit. The squid was once thirty-three feet long and weighed 1,091 pounds. I looked at it and gave a shiver but found myself looking closer and closer and walking around the exhibit examining every part of this weird creature. Its eye is eleven inches across. That's the size of a soccer ball!

Because Wellington is an easy city to explore on foot, on one visit I decided on one visit to park in the Kelburn neighborhood for the day. I took my time wandering down the hill and through the Botanical Gardens; I explored a new corner of Wellington then took the cable car up to my vehicle after I was ready to collapse from a full day of sightseeing.

I have always been fascinated by monarchies. I love fairytales starting with "Once upon a time in the kingdom of..." and I am intrigued with the Royal Family of England. Our next-door neighbors, Canada, pay allegiance to the queen of England, which has always left me with the question of "How does their government work?" New Zealand falls into the same category and this was a good opportunity to learn more.

New Zealand's system of government is described as a constitutional monarchy, which means that the Queen is the Head of State. Queen Elizabeth II was pronounced "Queen of this realm and all of her other realms" in 1952. She reigns over New Zealand independently from her position as Queen of England.

Parliament, whose job it is to make new laws, is made up of two parts: the Sovereign, who is the Queen, and the House of Representatives. In reality, the Queen has very little power—she is more of a figurehead. She must follow the rules of the constitution and has appointed a governor general to sign the bills.

The House of Representatives proposes and makes laws. Residents vote every three years for new members of parliament. To pass a new law a committee works on the bill. The bill is read two times to the House and revisions are made. The third reading is the final review before the law is passed. The Queen's representative then signs the law.

The governmental buildings have been in Wellington since 1865, making it the capital city. The Labours and Nationals are currently the two main parties.

The parliament complex housing the governmental buildings dominates several blocks of the city. Many different styles of architecture make it an interesting place to wander around. The Victorian gothic style of the Parliamentary Library is in stark contrast to the Parliament House, which is built of stone in the Edwardian neoclassical style. But the most recognizable building in the parliamentary complex is the Executive office building or the Beehive. Here most government ministers have their offices, as well as the Prime Minister, his department and Cabinet.

The name came from a box of "Beehive" brand matches that the architect, Sir Basil Spence, had been given. It stuck and the company later made special Beehive matchboxes for sale to MPs. Oddly his design does look like a traditional beehive and the buzz of activity commencing inside and around the building puts one in mind of a colony of workers and a queen bee directing the chaos.

Jokes have erupted over the years such as: "What's buzzing in the beehive?" or "We always knew our politicians spent most of their time going around in circles!"

The circular form of the building means that there are no rectangular rooms. The materials used in its construction are all from New Zealand. Since the Beehive is located on the Ring of Fire it uses the Base Isolation Earthquake Proofing system. This feat of engineering can absorb the impact of an earthquake up to 7.5 on the Richter scale and the building can move up to thirty centimeters in any horizontal direction. Numerous pillars located in the basement can shift in the event of an earthquake, minimizing damage to the building. The systems used in this design are now being used all over the world in high-risk areas.

I don't know if it was the charm, the water, the museums, the restaurants, or the All Blacks, but I found myself jumping into the car time and time again for the six hour drive to Mercer's 2014 Quality of Living, twelfth best city in the world.

Museum of New Zealand
Te Papa Tongarewa
55 Cable Street
http://www.tepapa.govt.nz/pages/default.aspx

Botanic Garden
http://wellington.govt.nz/recreation/gardens/botanic-garden/visitor-information

Wellington Cable Car
http://www.wellingtoncablecar.co.nz

Parliament building tours
http://www.parliament.nz/en-NZ/AboutParl/Visiting/

Its Fleece Was White as Snow

Spring is the time of year in New Zealand when new little lambs begin dotting the countryside like balls of cotton sprinkled on the lawn. Even if you live barely on the edge of town you have a few sheep in your yard because you are a Kiwi and that's what Kiwi's do.

Chad's office was amazing. They showed us every aspect of living in New Zealand and gave us every opportunity to try all the things this city family could never experience in the United States. One morning Chad's nurse, Josie, rang up to tell me in a very excited tone that she had located two baby lambs that were abandoned by their mum and needed a loving home.

"The American children must have this experience!" she insisted.

"What about the American Mom?" I wondered.

I am not a fan of adult animals but I do have a particularly weak spot for anything newborn and fuzzy. I am also a huge proponent of giving my kids every learning opportunity possible in life. So I agreed, and when the kids returned from school that day we piled into the car for "a big surprise." My kids picked up right away from my mumbling that although there was a surprise for them it was going to be more work for me!

We played a game of "guess what the surprise is" as we drove along the winding roads into the country. Somehow it was no surprise that sheep were involved. I guess they knew I was a bit over-the-top in love with the country and all these little animals bouncing around.

"Are we going to see some sheep?" asked Maddie.

"Are we going to feed some sheep?" asked Elena.

"Are we going to watch some sheep get docked?" asked Damon. Leave it to the boy to want to see the lambs be emasculated.

Laughing, I said a hearty "no" to all the questions as we pulled into the driveway. Four baby lambs were in a pen. The delighted kids got out and gently petted the newborns. Bottles were brought out and laughing floated through the air like a beautiful song as the lambs crowded in, greedily trying to get more than their fair share of food.

Then I told the kids they could pick two lambs to bring home. Excitement, joy and happiness poured from every fiber of their beings. Of course they picked the smallest two lambs. The tinier, the cuter—and the more needy.

You can only imagine our ride home. One mom focused on the curvy roads, three children full of excitement and two baby lambs, fresh from their mother's wombs, wrapped in towels and clutched in loving but eager arms on the kids' laps.

A stop in the agricultural store on the way home was in order. I had never graced the doors of this store before. It smelled like a farm and constituted shelves and shelves of country stuff.

How big of a bottle did I need? What nipple was best? How did I mix this formula and how many times a day did they need to eat? Put me in a Babies 'R Us with a new mom and I could advise on every necessary and unnecessary item to keep a baby healthy and content, but give me two lambs and I became helpless.

We finally headed home with a car weighed down with every necessity to raise two lambs including collars of different colors so that I could tell them apart and matching leashes so that the kids could parade their pets down the street.

Fortunately our yard was a maze of smaller yards, each blocked off with fences and gates. Small animals got a small space. As a worried mom I obsessed over them all night long, afraid that they would freeze to death in the wild outdoors. I never considered that my yard was much cleaner and more protected than the hills I had just rescued them from. Their little cries kept me awake and I got up with a major "bad mom" complex.

After bottle time in the morning I looked at the two dirty little fellows. I guess they weren't whisked away from their mom to be given a bath as soon as they entered into the world. That task would have to be up to us.

I filled the bathtub with a few inches of warm water while the kids carried the lambs inside. Giving a lamb a bath was a much more difficult job than giving a puppy a bath. It was like bathing a cat. Their little hooves slipped all over the porcelain bathtub, creating a swirl of muddy water. The floor filled with muddy puddles and the bathroom became a circus. The five of us all crowded in, trying to hold the wiggly animals, scrub them down and just offer helpful advice. Eventually they were clean, wrapped in towels and comforted in front of the fire. We now had two little lambs appropriate for city living with "fleece as white as snow."

Large discussions ensued concerning the naming of our two new family members. The kids figured out names using descriptions of physical characteristics. We landed on Tiny (for his size) and Hairy (for the silly looking tuft of hair growing out of the top of his head).

Our lambs grew quickly, gulping down their formula three times a day. They moved from the little yard into the big yard. I began to mutter, "Don't step in the poop," "Don't steal my clothes from the basket," and "It's not playtime yet." every time I hung out the laundry. Friends came over with their little kids to play with the lambs that jumped and bounced around our yard. A plaintive "baa" could be heard at all hours of the day and night. The kids were faithful with their jobs of caring for the pets. They were probably the most well loved and well cared for lambs in all of New Zealand.

In spite of the bath we learned that lamb tails are not cute and clean in real life. Paul and Josie stopped by to "dock" our little lambs for us. Docking is the job of cutting off the lamb's tail and putting a rubber band around his balls to keep them clean and free of disease. The rubber band slowly contracts, cutting off the blood supply, and in a few weeks the balls simply fall off the little lamb. This is all a bit shocking if you're not a farm girl.

The large stations in New Zealand have a docking season when extra help is hired for a few days to get the huge job done. This is one of the unique experiences Damon got to try. Part of the docking experience was "drenching" the lambs. Only in New Zealand can a family be watching a show on the telly and not think it is odd to advertise drenching medicines.

Josie flipped Hairy over and Paul clamped on the rubber bands, then they did the same to Tiny. In 60 seconds flat both lambs were hopping around the yard, kicking their legs, quite uncomfortable with their new situation.

Following a large docking, the Maoris collect the tails and have a party to grill them. Just the thought of a bucket of freshly cut dirty and slightly bloody tails is enough to turn my stomach. The long, skinny tails aren't particularly meaty so a good number are needed for a proper feast. The tails are grilled over an open fire until the wool is burnt off and the meat is cooked. The foul odor of burning wool can be smelt for miles around. They peel off the skin then nibble on the tasty meat. Think chicken wings—a lot of effort for very little reward. But just as in the culture of sitting around with a big pile of wings, greasy fingers, lots of beer and a football game playing in the background, so it is with lambs' tails.

Another three months into our lamb experience Josie stopped by for a visit. She noticed how the lambs were growing, barely staying confined in our little yard. Little did she know of the ordeal I endured by way of a friendly game of bull and matador in which I was the cape the lambs were trying to butt.

"It's time they move out to our station." And like that she whisked them off in her little car. How she made that drive home I can't even imagine.

When Tiny and Hairy were six months old we were informed that slaughter season was upon us. You can't let a lamb grow too old before killing it because otherwise you will be left with strong flavored meat that's also on the tough side of things.

One Saturday morning Chad put on some old clothes and drove over to Paul and Josie's. Paul slit the throat of the first lamb and Chad the second. Never having lived on a farm and not really having done much hunting, this was a difficult thing for him to do. I've always been proud of him for it. He knew our kids loved those little lambs. He helped feed them. Yet he understood that to live, something had to die.

Chad returned a few days later to pick up our meat, leaving a lamb for Paul and Josie for their trouble. That night as I pulled a luscious smelling roast, flavored with fresh rosemary out of the oven, the kids understood where the meat had come from. We are so clean in America, walking down a disinfected aisle to a refrigerated case to pick out our cellophane-wrapped meat. I was glad my children were learning a lesson in life about the reality of where food comes from.

Along with the meat came a large bag holding the skins of the two sheep. I peeked in. Dirty, bloody and stiff. I quickly closed the bag and lifted the lid to the chest freezer and stuffed the whole thing in to wait until my next trip to Napier.

Eventually the bag made it to the trunk of the car and into the *Classic Sheepskin Factory* in Napier. Six weeks later I picked up two gorgeous, soft, fluffy, white skins that now grace the backs of our furniture. They remind me of sunny afternoons frolicking in the backyard with three children and two little lambs.

Holidays

Life in a different country brought different customs, a different calendar, and a different rhythm to life. Gone was the Fourth of July celebration with fireworks lighting up the sky and a Thanksgiving feast that left one moaning on the couch in pain.

I found myself swimming in confusion as I tried to forego the customs I was used to while learning the traditions that brought cadence to this country. I learned that holidays and routine bring order to life. They define the calendar... Or maybe the calendar defines us. The history of events become a part of the people of the future.

The series of new-to-me holidays began January 2 with "The Day After New Years Day." Not only is the 1st a holiday but the next day as well. Apparently the new settlers from Britain and other parts of Europe were just as confused with summer falling during Christmas as I was. To help them adjust they added an extra day off work. Some Kiwis add more time to this to make a nice long midsummer break.

April 25 brought ANZAC Day or "Australian and New Zealand Army Corps Day." This holiday commemorates the first major action fought by Australia and New Zealand during the First World War. The soldiers, nicknamed "Anzacs," fought the battle of Gallipoli in Turkey on April 25, 1915. Strong support by those back home was given to the soldiers that were now fully engaged in the war. The battle was meant to open the Black Sea passage for the Allies but it turned into a major disaster. Met with strong resistance, the battle lasted eight long months. Although both sides suffered major casualties, eight thousand Australians and two thousand seven hundred New Zealanders were killed. The forces from New Zealand distinguished themselves with their display of courage and skill while forging an enduring bond with the Australians they fought alongside. In the ninth month the campaign was abandoned and the surviving troops evacuated. Close to one-third of the New Zealanders involved had been killed.

Rather than celebrating victory in battle, New Zealand remembers the bond that was forged with Australia and the distinct identity they established in the eyes of the world with their bravery, ingenuity, and loyalty.

We often commented on how little patriotism we saw observed in daily life throughout New Zealand, so we were startled with the sudden display of patriotism around us. War songs were sung; documentaries televised; announcements were in the paper and assemblies at the schools.

I attended the ANZAC Day memorial service at the local War Memorial Hall. As I walked in with the kids, two WWI planes flew over, and retired soldiers entered. In a ceremony rich with tradition, I felt a little awkward not knowing what the protocol was. When was I supposed to stand and when should I sit? Did I join in with the singing or remain quiet? How should I dress and where did everyone get the paper poppies they were wearing?

During the 1920's, New Zealanders began to wear a red poppy in remembrance for the men and women who died serving their country. Throughout history, red poppies have signified fallen service men. A flash of red pinned to your clothes reminds you of the blood men sacrificed for freedom, fighting these wars. The tradition began during the Napoleonic Wars of the early nineteenth century. Later in the same region of France and Belgium, red poppies were associated with those who died during World War I. Lieutenant Colonel John McCrae, MD of the Canadian Army, penned his famous poem in 1915 after enduring seventeen days of hell. Having buried a young friend and former student the day before, he gazed across the cemetery at the wild poppies blowing in a gentle eastern wind.

In Flanders Fields
By John McCrae

In Flanders Fields the poppies blow
Between the crosses row on row,
That mark our place; and in the sky
The larks, still bravely singing, fly
Scarce heard amid the guns below.

We are the Dead. Short days ago
We lived, felt dawn, saw sunset glow,
Love and were loved, and now we lie

In Flanders fields.

Take up our quarrel with the foe;
To you from failing hands we throw
The torch; be yours to hold it high.
If ye break faith with us who die
We shall not sleep, though poppies grow
In Flanders fields. [6]

Similar to a war funeral, the service began with singing "God Save the Queen." The local priest led the service with a prayer, reading scripture and singing the twenty-third Psalm. The mayor, dressed in a traditional Maori feather cape, followed with an address. The local Lions Club sang old wartime songs. The older generation joined right in, their voices wavering in the air. Military representatives from Australia and New Zealand gave speeches commemorating the brotherhood of the two countries.

Outside at a memorial, cadets stood in respect. City officials stood with retired military personnel and an active military fireguard gathered around the flag as it was lowered then raised again during a bugle call. Wreaths were lovingly laid on the memorial and a twenty-one-gun salute echoed in the air. Following the service many in the community placed white crosses around the memorial.

I was given a glimpse into the heart of a nation and saw what it holds dear. The pride of fighting in a world war and the sorrow for the lost has not died over the years.

Even though the Queen lives far away in another hemisphere, her birthday is celebrated around the world. As a constitutional monarchy, New Zealand joins in the holiday on the first Monday of June. Because it is a public holiday, government is closed as well as many businesses. Ignorant of this day, I found myself in Gisborne a bit discouraged at the wasted trip. A good meal was about all that came out of the day for me.

Remember, remember the fifth of November.
Gunpowder, Treason and Plot.
I see no reason why Gunpowder Treason
Should ever be forgot. [7]

This little rhyme is chanted by kids to remember Guy Fawkes. It is not an official holiday, but nonetheless important in the eyes of New Zealanders. As odd as the name is, so is the story surrounding the man. English Catholics had been persecuted for many years under the rule of King James the First. A group of twelve men placed gunpowder under the House of Lords in England. Hopes of greater religious freedom had faded and those involved in the Gunpowder Plot desired renewed attention. On November 5, 1605, Guy Fawkes, a member of the Gunpowder Plot, was found guarding thirty six barrels of gunpowder intended to reduce the House of Lords to rubble. He was arrested, tried, convicted of high treason and sentenced to be hung, drawn and quartered. Just before his execution he leapt from the scaffold and broke his neck.

Bonfires are lit and effigies of Guy Fawkes are burned to celebrate the failure of Fawkes and the safety of the king. Old clothes are stuffed with newspaper to make dummies that look like men. Communities often close the night with an ironic fireworks display.

In our community the celebrations were limited to families. We were invited to our friend's, Ian and Theresa's, home where the kids ran around with sparklers and lit off a heap of fireworks. I left confused, not able to wrap my mind around the celebration of a hanged man.

The last holiday to give me a start was December 26, Boxing Day. After inquiring among my friends I was led to believe this was a holiday to simply fold the boxes that held the gifts given on Christmas Day and pack them away to be reused the next year. Although it sounded a bit goofy, I ran with it.

In reality, Boxing Day seems to have many different origins and significances. It could be in tradition of the day when servants and tradespeople received their gifts from employers, or it could be a holiday when banks were closed but shops were open advertising heavy sales. It is also St. Stephen's Day when the first martyr in the Christian faith is remembered. Another traditional use of the day was to get rid of old clothes and household items, pack them into boxes and distribute them to the poor. Regardless of the origin, it was a day off.

Christmas

City sidewalks, busy sidewalks.
Dressed in holiday style
In the air
There's a feeling
of Christmas[8]

I read these words, close my eyes and hear Bing Crosby's voice sing the melody. Warmth, safety and happiness reach into the depths of my soul. In the first few lines of a simple tune I find myself lost in another world. I love Christmas and all the associations that go with it—snow, pine trees, red and green, food, music, sweaters and decorations. Memories of times with family and friends come alive once again.

New Zealand took all identification I had with Christmas and threw it out the window. Rather than anticipating a school Christmas program and holiday classroom parties for the kids, we had End of the Year Prize Givings and summer kick-offs. Lights were strung-up downtown but they didn't turn on until 8:30 p.m.—long before sunset. It was hard to pop into the coffee shop to enjoy a bit of air-conditioning and hear Frosty the Snowman playing over the speakers. It just didn't jive with me.

Ask a Kiwi what they associate with Christmas and with a far off look in their eye they will share the joy of summer bbq's, Christmas morning at the bach, a day on the beach and Christmas Fruit Cake. Take away these events and they would feel as lost as I did.

I tried hard to look beyond my preconceived notions of Christmas to find new ways to celebrate and claim the season as my own. The beauty of living in a small town was that I had the opportunity to move from observing traditions to becoming a participant. The town asked me to be one of the judges for the float competition in the annual Christmas/Summer parade. Businesses, associations and groups threw themselves into costumes and decorations of all sorts. It was a festive affair on all accounts. Of course, a small town really only produces a small parade, so the tradition was that when it reached the traffic circle at the end of the main street, the line continued right around and returned for a second showing. More waving hands and throwing of candy brought in the Christmas season with a flourish.

Motivated to create a real Christmas for my family, I set up a borrowed Christmas tree in the family room. About three feet high, it was truly the most classic Charlie Brown-ish tree I had ever had. The bright tinsel branches resurrected from the 50's welcomed the origami ornaments that Maddie had created. A few paper chains strung around the house completed our meager Christmas decor.

Christmas helped me embrace the small town we lived in. The familiarity of strolling down the main street and greeting those I knew began to bring a homey warmth into my heart. I had been there long enough to feel like a local, a part of the community.

Wairoa had a charming tradition shortly before Christmas. Carols in the Park was a time when the community spread their blankets on the banks of the river next to the old lighthouse in the early throws of twilight. Together we sang Christmas carols and listened to the Christmas story. I lit my candle as the sun began to sink below the horizon. I was surrounded by friends. Leaning my head back on the blanket in contentment, the sky lit up in its own glorious display of Christmas lights. A lone bagpiper stood at the base of the lighthouse. His melody drifted across the river as each person walked toward home with warm thoughts of the day soon to come.

One thing I love to do each Christmas is to bake heaps of cookies. I have about thirteen different varieties that I save solely for this time of year. Every gathering includes a plate of cookies carefully decorated. Yes, every American knows this tradition and has probably participated in a Christmas cookie exchange at some point in time. New Zealanders are not as fond of sweets as Americans. They usually prefer a savory appetizer, but they are quite proud of their "Christmas Cake." About six weeks before Christmas people began to soak fruit in brandy for their cake. The tradition is taken quiet seriously. One would never dream of using the cake as a weapon or re-gifting it to another person. Conversations commenced with whispers on the progress of their fruitcake. Generation after generation passes their recipe down. When the opportunity arose, I tasted a bite, then passed it on to let others enjoy the fruit of their labors.

God gave his own Christmas decoration to New Zealand in the form of the pohutukawa tree. Found along the coasts of the North Island, this native evergreen produces a brilliant red flower in December. The flower is made of hundreds of delicate red needles that reminded me of a circus toy. Filaments light up a florescent wand that childen wave in glee. The Maori place importance on this tree in the legend of Tawhaki. As a young warrior he attempted to climb to heaven to find help in seeking revenge for his father's death. Tragically, he fell to earth. The crimson flowers are said to symbolize his blood.

Despite my attempts to create a Christmas in New Zealand, I could never completely accept the differences, so we decided to pack up the car and head north for a week. If we weren't going to have snow, we wanted to have the most opposite experience possible—sun and sand.

The Night Before Christmas - Kiwi Style
by Yvonne Morrison

It was the night before Christmas, and all round the bach
Not a possum was stirring; not one we could catch.
We left on the table a meat pie and beer,
In hopes that Santa Claus soon would be here.
We children were snuggled up in our bunk beds,
While dreams of pavlova danced in our heads;
And mum in her nightie, and dad in his shorts,
Had just settled down to watch TV sports.
When outside the bach such a ho-ha arose,
I woke up at once from my wonderful doze.
I ran straight to the sliding door, looking about,
Jumped out on the deck, and let out a shout.
The fairy lights dad had strung up around the door
Let me see everything down to the shore.
And what did I see, when I took a peep?
But a miniature tractor and eight tiny sheep.
With a little old driver, his dog on his knee.
I knew at once who this joker might be.
He patted his dog, and in a voice not unkind,
Cried "Good on ya, boy! Now, get in behind!"
"Now, Flossy! now Fluffy! now Shaun and Shane!
On, Bossy! on, Buffy on, Jason and Wayne!
Up that red tree, to the top of the bach!
But mind you don't trample the vegetable patch."
So up on the roof those sheep quickly flew,
With the tractor of toys, Santa and his dog too.
As my sister awoke and I turned around,
In through the window he came with a bound.
He wore a black singlet and little white shorts,
And stuck on his feet were gumboots of course;
A sack full of toys he had flung on his back,
And he looked like a postie just opening his pack.
His eyes bright as paua shell- oh, how they twinkled!

Like an old tuatara, his skin was all wrinkled!
He had a wide face and a round, fat tummy,
That looked like he'd eaten lots that was yummy.
He spoke not a word, but got down on one knee,
And placed a cricket set under the tree,
A present for sis, one for dad, one for mum,
Then he turned and he winked and held up his thumb.
He jumped on his tractor, to his dog gave a whistle,
And away they all flew, as fast as a missile.
I called out "thanks," as he flew past the gate.
He called back: "Kia ora to all, and good on ya, mate."[9]

The Night Before Christmas
By Yovvone Morrison
Children's book
http://www.paperplus.co.nz/book/kiwi-night-before-christmas-9781869439156

Classic Christmas Cake

450 grams currants
180 grams raisins
180 grams sultanas
75g finely chopped mixed peel
1/4 cup brandy
225 grams butter, softened
225 grams soft brown sugar
4 eggs, at room temperature
225 grams plain flour
1/4 tsp salt
1/2 tsp grated nutmeg (more spice to mask the flavor)
1/2 tsp mixed spice
75g chopped, blanched almonds
1 Tbs treacle
Finely grated zest of 1 orange
35 grams whole blanched almonds, to decorate

1. The day (or month) before baking, place dried fruit, mixed peel and brandy in large bowl. Mix well and cover with plastic wrap. Leave for 24 hours, stirring occasionally. Line a 20 cm round cake tin or 18 cm square tin with brown paper and a lining of nonstick baking paper.

2. Next day, heat oven to 140°C (120°C fan bake). Place butter and sugar in a large bowl and beat with an electric mixer until pale and fluffy. Beat in eggs one at a time, beating well between each addition.

3. Sift flour, salt and spices together and gently fold into beaten mixture. Fold in brandy-soaked fruit, chopped almonds, treacle and orange zest. Spoon the mixture into prepared cake tin, spreading it evenly and smoothing the surface with the back of a spoon.

4. Decorate surface with whole almonds. Bake for 3 to 3 1/2 hours or until an inserted skewer comes out clean. If necessary, cover loosely with foil part way through cooking to prevent over-browning. Cool in cake tin for 1 hour, then remove to a wire rack to cool completely.

* Traditional Christmas fruitcakes are best made well in advance - at the end of October or beginning of November - so the flavors can mature.

* "Feed" the cake with brandy about once a week by making holes all over the cake with a skewer, then spooning over brandy to soak through the holes and permeate the cake with flavor.

* To store, wrap the cake in a double layer of greaseproof paper, then wrap it again in foil or place in an airtight cake tin. Don't wrap in plastic wrap or the cake will sweat and deteriorate.[10]

Auckland

People encouraged us to head north for the holidays to ensure a break with sun and sand. We took them up on this advice and hopped into the car for the six-hour drive to Auckland.

It had been six months since we stepped off the plane in Auckland not knowing what to expect. Things that were new and foreign then had become run-of-the-mill and common now. The settled-in feeling gave us an opportunity to see Auckland through rested eyes, able to take in our surroundings.

Auckland is the largest city in New Zealand with 1.4 million residents—still only a drop in the bucket compared to other large cities in the world. In 2014, Mercer Quality of Living ranked Auckland third on its list of "best cities to live in the world." Auckland has a feeling of business in contrast to Wellington's more charming quality.

The city has a lot to offer. The Auckland Zoo is home to the largest collection of native and exotic animals in New Zealand. The Auckland War Memorial Museum, also simply called Auckland Museum, is located in a beautiful neoclassical building that houses the most extensive Maori and Pacific Island collection in the country. The focus of this museum is on New Zealand's natural history and military history. The Court of Honor in front of the museum is a memorial to those who lost their lives in the First and Second World Wars. The Voyager Maritime Museum focuses on New Zealand's important relationship with the sea. A unique ride on the harbor in one of the museum's historic boats can be booked in advance. Whether you want to hike or kayak, Auckland offers many opportunities to get outdoors. Because a city can't be taken seriously in New Zealand without offering adventure sports, you can take a wild motor boat ride or jump six hundred thirty feet from New Zealand's highest building, the Sky Tower.

But our family felt that we had a pretty good feel for New Zealand's history and culture by this point so we bypassed the museums and attractions to wander the streets. We walked past the giant Christmas baubles in Aotea Square, posing next to the oversized ornaments for photos. We spent over an hour gazing into the windows of Smith & Caughey at the intricately detailed displays. Each year a different Christmas story comes to life through small mechanized figures set against fabulous backdrops. We walked around the building, absorbing the story as it unfolded in various scenes. I felt like I had stepped into the magical land of a fairytale. Whitcoulls' creepy Santa caught our attention as well. The sixty-six foot tall jolly man has stood guard over Whitcoulls bookstore since 1960. We couldn't help but stare at his winking eye and motorized finger beckoning us closer. Instinctively I put a protective arm around my daughters as we turned to go. A shiver quietly worked its way up my spine. Despite a recent makeover on Santa, he still made the top of Cracked's list deeming him the most "unintentionally creepy Christmas ornament."

Sometimes you just need to get out of the city. Hop onto Fullers Passenger Ferry and in ten minutes you'll find yourself in the quaint sea village of Devonport, a town full of art galleries, boutiques and gift shops. The journey is as glorious as the destination. The wind blew through my hair as I stood at the rail on the ferry. I took in the beautiful views of the city skyline as we pulled away from shore. The Sky Needle grew separate the further away we floated until it became a distinct symbol representing the city. The hustle and bustle of the large city seemed remote as I stepped ashore at Devonport. We spent a lovely afternoon wandering the Victorian streets, eating at cafes and perusing shops before we boarded the ferry for the return trip.

Auckland Zoo
Motions Road
Western Springs
Auckland
www.aucklandzoo.co.nz

Auckland War Memorial Museum
Museum Circuit
Parnell, Auckland
www.aucklandmuseum.com

Fullers Ferry
99 Quay Street (at the bottom of Queen Street)
www.fullers.co.nz

Skycity
Cnr Victoria and Federal St.
Auckland Central
www.skycityauckland.co.nz/attractions/skytwoer.html

Voyager New Zealand Maritime Museum
Located on the corner of Quay and Hobson Streets in the heart of the Viaduct Harbour.
www.maritimemuseum.co.nz

<u>Bay of Islands</u>

Another day in the car took us out of Auckland and further north. Northland is the most northern of the sixteen regions of New Zealand. Beginning on the outskirts of Auckland, the rolling hills are farmed and forested. Long, sandy beaches stretch along the western side of this peninsula. The climate is mild with warm, humid summers and wet winters.

Whangarei Falls was a good place to stop and stretch our legs before arriving at our final destination of Paihia. A short thirty-minute loop took us past the eighty-five foot falls. The kids were delighted to run and climb on the rocks.

The Bay of Islands is a popular tourist destination. Located on the east coast, close to the northern tip of New Zealand it offers great weather, sailing and fishing. Beloved author Zane Grey was enthralled by the beauty and spectacular scenery of the Bay of Islands over ninety years ago. White sand beaches, wineries and orchards fill this narrow strip of land. Dolphins play in the waves and around the one hundred fifty islands— many of which remain relatively unexplored.

This is where the first European settlers arrived. The Declaration of Independence from England was signed here as well as the Treaty of Waitangi. It is a very important historical area of the country and we wanted to round off our education with a visit to Waitangi. The treaty grounds were a gift given to the nation of New Zealand to preserve this important part of their history. The Treaty House was the house of the first British resident, James Busby.

Busby was a bit of an interesting character. Born and raised in Scotland, he moved as a young adult to Australia with his parents. In and out of jobs in Liverpool and Australia, he dabbled with vine growing and trained in Europe as a viticulturist. On a trip to England in 1831 he impressed the Colonial Office with information on various colonial matters including New Zealand. He believed that New Zealand was an example of 'extreme frontier chaos.' This gained him an appointment in New Zealand as British Resident. He moved to Waitangi in 1833 and the following year his wife joined him. He built a two-room residence and planted the vine stock he had collected in Europe. He wasn't given any resources or power, yet was instructed to protect settlers and traders, prevent European outrages against the Maori, and arrest escaped convicts. Despite a lack of support and even a bit of disdain, Busby managed to unite the country under one flag, and create a Declaration of Independence. Thirty-four chiefs signed the document and it became a significant mark of Maori national identity. This move thwarted the French plan to make New Zealand a French sovereignty. The crown finally listened to Busby's pleas for aid in settling the outbreaks of tribal fighting and sent William Hobson in 1837. Hobson helped reduce the tensions and returned to England proposing that British sovereignty be established over New Zealand. Busby and Hobson worked together to draft the Treaty of Waitangi which was signed at his home. While in position in Waitangi, Busby began farming and trading. He imported sheep and developed a vineyard, vegetable gardens and a forest nursery. He purchased land with great plans of a town for new settlers, but his scheme did not take off so he returned to Australia.

His house, named Te Whare Runanga, a representative Maori meetinghouse, and Ngatokimatawhaorua, a large Maori ceremonial war canoe, are also located on the grounds. Walking through these places, reading the history, touching the Maori carvings and recalling all that we had experienced thus far brought the history of the country together for us.

We stopped for lunch at the much acclaimed Mangonui Fish Shop to see if they really were "New Zealand's best fish and chips." The location is fabulous with the restaurant cantilevered over the water. Small boats came and went while we enjoyed a greasy meal of fish. In my opinion the food didn't come close to the melt-in-your-mouth fish and chips I had become used to in our little town of Wairoa.

Christmas Eve awoke bright and clear as we drove another ninety minutes north to Cape Reinga at the tippy-top of the North Island. The Maori word, reinga, means "underworld." The Maori believe that this is the place where the spirits of the dead enter into the underworld. It's easy to believe this as you look down at the swirling waters where the Tasman Sea and the Pacific Ocean collide. We walked out to the white lighthouse signaling the end of the island. The wind caught our hair, twirling it into tangles as it churned the sea below. Only behind us could a thin strip of land be seen. Surrounded by the vastness of the water I realized what a long distance I had traveled to stand in this spot. Not just from our little town of Wairoa, but from home in Michigan where our family would gather around the Christmas tree, share a meal and attend the Christmas Eve service.

Our next stop was the sand dunes at Te Paki Stream at the north end of Ninety Mile Beach. Mountains of fine, golden sand greeted us as we looked west towards the sea. The only other time I had seen anything like these dunes was in Northern Michigan at the Sleeping Bear Dunes. The dunes were an important meeting place for the Maori to fish and collect shellfish. Wild and untamed, the dunes loomed in front of us. A small booth at the bottom of the dune was renting boogie boards. We decided to save a few bucks and tucked our cheap store-bought boards under our arms. A few people dotted the slopes as we slowly trudged up, pulling the boards behind. We collapsed to rest in the sand and enjoyed the victory of arrival. Running, jumping and diving in one fluid motion, the kids were on their way down the mountain of sand. We quickly discovered that our cheap boards created too much friction on the sand as the kids puttered down the hill, pushing at the sand with their hands. Elena had left the plastic wrapping on hers so she flew past her siblings with great speed. I could hear her screams as the plastic ripped causing the board to stop and Elena to go airborne. Flying sand and screeches of thrill filled the air as she tumbled and rolled to a stop. We broke down and rented a couple boards, then headed back up the hill. This time we soared down the mountain. We had races and cheered one another on. I watched many attempts before giving it a go. I ran and landed in a belly-flop on my board. I was flying at lightning speed. Suddenly I was going faster than my board was. In a tangle of arms and legs I rolled in the sand half way down the slope like tumbleweed in the desert. It was all good sandy fun and we were completely exhausted when we turned in the boards.

We decided to take the beach route back to the hotel. I was a nervous wreck the entire drive which completely ruined all hopes of enjoying the experience. 90 Mile Beach has a reputation for driving cars on the sand. I had been on the Internet reading all the tips and warnings. I was sure we had not timed the high tide correctly and would be washed away, never to be seen again. I was afraid we would hit soft sand and become stuck with no one to rescue us until high tide when we would be swept out to sea. But I didn't need to worry. The beach was completely deserted as far as we could see in any direction. Not a house, a car or a person. We stopped and walked on the shore while the kids played with the skim board in the water. We danced and romped as the sun began to sink. When we pulled off the beach and onto the road I looked back at the ocean for one last glimpse. I could swear I saw a sleigh pulled by eight tiny reindeer in the sky across the ocean coming to welcome Christmas to New Zealand.

As Christmas Day peeked above the horizon, I laid presents out for the kids. It would be a small gift giving year because I knew not much would make it home to the States. We had tried several times to find a market open Christmas Eve to pick up food for the day, but New Zealand shuts down when the sun disappears. I opened the refrigerator and gazed inside. Christmas Day is a time when a mother provides for her family. Mounds of sweet treats and a large, special meal need to be laid on the table. Only the irresponsible woman would not have this for her family. Looking into the empty cavity I realized that we might be having a feast of peanut butter and jelly if no restaurants were open. My hopes were not high considering the lack of business the day before. The scene from "A Christmas Story" where the family is alone, eating Christmas dinner in a Chinese restaurant did not seem so funny as it loomed before me as a possibility.

The kids enjoyed their small pile of gifts, but when you are very far away from home with only yourselves to share the day with, any thought from an outside person becomes monumental. One box had arrived in Wairoa before we left. We packed it in the already overstuffed car and toted it North with us. The kids opened the box on Christmas morning to find graham crackers, Hershey's candy bars and jet-puffed marshmallows. Everything we needed to make s'mores! Their faces glowed and a tear trickled down my cheek at the thoughtfulness of my friend. Here in a hotel room with gifts from friends, suddenly home didn't seem as far away as it had the day before when I had gazed across the wide, open ocean.

Our hotel in Paihia was about a five-minute drive out of town on the Waitangi Lagoon overlooking the Haruru Falls. Dressed in swimsuits, we hired kayaks and paddled our way out into the lagoon. This was not the typical Christmas Day activity of making snowmen that I was used to. The sun beat down on us as we floated to the horseshoe shaped falls, our skin cooled by the spray. As I slipped under the falls, the fifteen-foot cascade poured on my head and soaked me with refreshing water. A pohutukawa tree leaned over the cliff raining down its brilliant red Christmas flowers.

In town we played on the beach before finding a pizza restaurant open for business. Christmas did not meet my preconceived notions of what the day should look and feel like, but I've found that when I'm able to push those expectations aside I find a beautiful gift waiting for me.

Auckland's leading export in the early 19th century was kauri gum. The fossilized resin from kauri trees, a form of amber, was originally used by the Maoris for chewing, tattooing, fire starting and jewelry. The kauri tree is New Zealand's largest native tree. It is a type of hardwood conifer which grows in subtropical regions. A resin leaks through cracks in the bark or an injury in the tree and hardens when exposed to air. The lumps often fall to the ground, eventually fossilizing.

Someone discovered that kauri gum was a particularly useful ingredient in commercial varnish. In the 1840's exports began to London and America. Gum fields were mainly located in Auckland, Northland and Coromandel where the kauri forests flourished. European immigrants joined the Maoris in walking through the woods and swamps to collect the gum that had fallen to the forest floor. Within ten years the ground was picked clean. Men turned to shovels and spears to harvest the gum and the term "gum-digger" was coined. Gum digging was low paying and extremely hard work. The diggers, including women and children, were transient people. The fields were often found in swamps or scrubby areas, making their work tedious. By the 1890's, twenty thousand people were scraping a living together as gum-diggers. The outbreak of World War I brought a halt to the industry, followed by a small revival at the conclusion of the war. The work force struggled and is no longer existent. The kauri forests were eventually timbered and turned into farmland. Today only four percent of the kauri forests remain.

The Kauri Museum in Northland displays the complete history of the gumming industry. The largest kauri tree is found in the Waipoua Forest. Long and short hiking trails wind through the forest. The famous Tane Mahuta kauri tree is around 2,000 years old, fourteen feet five inches in diameter and fifty-eight feet high; it may be one of the largest trees you will ever see in your life.

As I thought about the gum tree industry in the early years of New Zealand, I wondered about the term "gumboots." Known in America as "rain boots" and in England as "wellingtons," every resident of this country owns a pair. It was not uncommon to see a man in shorts and a t-shirt walking down the street wearing the black rubber boots or to have a friend grab a pair out of the back seat of their car before a hike. Women hang their clothes on the line using them to keep their feet dry and clean, and children wear them to school. Gumboot day is celebrated in Taihape and comedian John Clark wrote "The Gumboot Song." There may not actually be much association between the kauri tree and a New Zealand gumboot. The name refers to the gum harvested from rubber trees to make the boots. Friends told me that the gum diggers wore black rubber knee boots when working in the swamps, but I couldn't find any hard proof of this.

Travel.CNN lists Middle Arch in Poor Knights Islands, New Zealand number eighteen on its list of the fifty best dive sites in the world. Located fourteen miles east off the Tutkaka Coast, the waters of Poor Knights Islands marine preserve are warmed by currents swept south from the Coral Sea. Subtropical fish living in the preserve are not found anywhere else in New Zealand. Underwater wonders such as sponge gardens and gorgonian fields provide life for a myriad of fish, shellfish, urchins and anemones. Divers can explore drop offs, walls, caves, arches and tunnels. The world's largest sea cave, Rikoriko, is on the northwest side of the island. During World War II, a Japanese submarine hid inside the cave for two weeks while undergoing repairs. Another world awaits you, whether diving or not, inside the cave.

Haruru Falls Resort
Bottom of Old Wharf Road
Haruru Falls
www.harurufalls.co.nz

Kauri Museum
5 Church Road
R.D.1
Matakohe
Northland
www.kauri-museum.com

Mangonui Fish Shop
Beach Rd.
Mangonui

Waipoua Forest
West coast of Dargaville
Northland
www.doc.govt.nz

Waitangi Treaty Grounds
From Auckland take SH1 North through Paihia. At the roundabout follow the signs.
www.waitangi.net.nz

A New Day Has Come

New Year's Eve is not something I typically get overly excited about. In fact, I can really only remember two past New Year's Eves: 1990, the year I was a Senior in high school and had a party at my house, and Y2K with all the hype of the new millennium. That year we celebrated with friends at our little house in Capac, Michigan. So, it was about time to have another memorable experience, and what better place than the East coast of New Zealand?

I had a few brief moments when I considered the idea of driving ninety minutes up to Gisborne to celebrate, because it is the first city in the world to see the sun of the New Year. (This could be argued as there are a few cities in some of the Pacific Islands that are closer to the international dateline, but due to the earth's tilt on its axis on New Year's Day, Gisborne wins.) I quickly dismissed those thoughts as the idea of being on the beach in a crowd of noisy, drunken people was not really how I envisioned welcoming in my New Year. Good friends and a deserted beach were a bit more what I had in mind.

On New Year's Eve Ruth and Russell came over. None of us are big on the New Year's Eve thing so we popped in a movie and figured we would call it an early night. We enjoyed an evening watching the movie and eating Key Lime Pie. The movie ended at 11:30, and since we were so close to the New Year that we sort of hung around until midnight entertaining ourselves with YouTube videos. Uneventfully, midnight came, we said our cheers and headed to bed.

The alarm rang, as Ruth would say, at a sparrow's fart (4:30 am). We got dressed, snuck out of the house—leaving the kids sleeping— picked up Ruth and Russell, and headed to the beach five minutes away. The sun was already beginning to lighten the sky with a deep orange band of color. We found a large washed up tree to sit on, cuddled up to our mate and sipped coffee. We were alone. Not another soul was on the beach. The ocean was peaceful and calm with small waves rolling ashore. The sky was clear with a smattering of clouds. The show of color that unfolded before us in the next hour was breathtaking. We spoke in a hush, respecting the serenity of the moment. Color exploded before us like silent fireworks, lighting up the sky and then silently morphing into other hues and shades. We felt an electricity of anticipation watching for the sun to burst over the horizon. We finally breathed deeply as she triumphantly emerged, bringing the first day of the New Year.

Not quite ready to let go of the moment and jump into a new day, Ruth and Russell came over for breakfast. We pulled egg casserole and cinnamon rolls out of the oven, squeezed some fresh orange juice, made coffee drinks, sat outside and enjoyed one another's company for the next few hours.

I may have been five minutes behind those in Gisborne to see the New Year, but nothing can compare to the deserted beach and spectacular light show that I shared with those close to me that morning.

A&P Show

Settled back into our little home in Wairoa, the summer loomed in front of us. Lazy days were spent at the beach in Mahia, but what summer is complete without a fair? Part of a traditional American upbringing, the county fair consists of 4H barns filled with animals, carnies showing how easy it would be to win their game if you just slap $2.00 on the table, the smell of deep fried elephant ears, and the twinkle of lights on the ferris wheel as it goes round and round late into the night. I felt as if I had stepped back in time watching the events of the fair in Wairoa as people showcased the skills they used every day on their stations. In New Zealand the fair is called the A&P show—Agriculture and Pastoral.

The kids and I headed over on a Friday afternoon with the rest of our little town to catch the opening horse events. We met some friends from England and looked in amazement at the spread they had set out to nibble on all afternoon. This was a far cry from brats and greasy fries sold from a noisy box on wheels. A blanket was laid on the grass with a wicker basket in the center bursting with crackers, cheese and grapes. A bottle of wine sat next to the basket complete with stemware. The Europeans really know how to picnic in style. We settled on the blankets and enjoyed a lazy summer afternoon under a big tree watching English style riding, dressage, and jumping.

Later in the evening, Chad joined us to watch the speed shearing competition. What fun! New Zealand is known for having some of the top professional sheep shearers in the world. The timer began. The sheep seemed to give up life and go limp when the shearers grabbed them and began shearing. Had I been on the stage, there would have been a mess of legs and fur, lots of bleating and a general look of a battle being fought. Loud music got everyone into the atmosphere as the announcer, sounding a bit like an auctioneer, yelled out times and placements. Like magic, the sheep was suddenly standing on four legs once again, feeling naked and exposed with its fur in a pile on the floor. The winner sheared his sheep in only nineteen seconds! The next day sheep shearing continued with team events and timed trials to see how many sheep one person could shear in a set time period.

On Saturday morning we fought the crowds (ok no crowds, this is Wairoa!) to get into the fairgrounds to see the horse show that we Americans could identify with—the Rodeo! Steer wrestling, barrel racing and calf roping were all done in Western style. Some ranchers still use horses to round up their sheep, although many have switched over to four-wheelers.

Taking a break from the sun, we headed into the domestics barn and found several women spinning wool fleece into yarn. More women were in rocking chairs knitting the yarn into sweaters. A room nearby had the fleece entrants and the winners. Sheep seemed to be a large focus of the A&P show.

I also had an entry in the domestics' barn. I had been working on a Crazy Quilt for the past year and a half, that I finished just two weeks before the A&P show. Some friends suggested that I enter the quilt into the competition. What fun to win first place in patchwork! Well, there wasn't very much competition, but it was still a very rewarding experience. I was beginning to feel like I really fit into this little town.

Just outside the domestics barn the "iron man" competition was going on. Teams of three had to do a variety of events including sheep shearing, wood chopping, hay bale rolling, pig carrying and other such things.

As we headed back towards the main strip we stopped to watch the dog trials. I had learned that a good dog is essential to the smooth operation of a farm. The farmer relies on his dogs to round up the sheep and cows. A well-trained dog takes a large investment of time. Each trial took between ten and fifteen minutes as the dog steered a group of sheep through a course. It was fascinating to watch these dogs work the sheep. The master typically carried a cane. He rarely lifted the cane, but occasionally used it to create a visual barrier, causing the sheep to walk in a different direction. The sheep were truly not interested in walking through a course. They would much rather eat grass. The patience of the farmer was amazing as well.

To finish up our day we watched some wood chopping. If you won a round of wood chopping you entered the next round with a nine second penalty. The man we had our eye on had just won four rounds, giving him a twenty-seven second penalty. There was a three-way tie for first in this round. We held our breath as the men drove their axes with steel power into the wood, willing the log to split and determine a winner. Chips of wood flew into the air as the men chopped at their logs. Sweat spilled off their faces as the sun beat down. In less than a minute it was all over. A champion had been named.

Satisfied from a full day, we dragged our tired selves back to the car for the five-minute drive home.

Always Something to Do

Even though Wairoa was such a little, out of the way town, there was always some type of entertainment going on. A group would pass through on their circuit from little town to little town, or the city would come up with some sort entertainment on its own.

All summer people talked about the horse races, claiming that they were THE social event in town. Not knowing a thing about horse races, we decided to just go and see what all the fuss was about.

I was a bit surprised at the number of cars when we arrived. I didn't know there were that many people in the area. Yes, indeed, everyone in town had come out for the day. Many appeared quite early to claim a front row seat. They found a perfect spot to set up their tents— complete with a lace-covered table, wicker picnic basket, wine and hors d'oeuvres. It was a bit of a fashion show as well. Some of us were in shorts and t-shirts while others were dressed to the hilt wearing a summer lawn dress, spiffy hairdo and arm linked with their dapper partner. Shouts of "hello" and a wave of the hand made everyone feel welcome.

The announcer rattled off names and statistics of the horses, encouraging everyone to get in line and place their bets. Wairoa did quite well that day, raking in a pleasing $1,000,000 plus in profits.

The races themselves were quite fun to watch. The jockeys warmed up in a ring and then filed out when it was their turn to race. The horses whinnied and shifted anxiously in anticipation of the run. They lined up at the gate and the gun went off. The hoofs thundered past, leaving a cloud of dust while the announcer yelled the leaders' names. The cows grazing in the center didn't seem to be bothered by all the commotion. It was a great day of walking around and socializing while watching the races. We had fun guessing who would win, inspecting the grooming and looking at the jockeys' uniforms.

True to Wairoa tradition, many kids had a piece of cardboard in tow and spent the afternoon sliding down the hill while their parents watched the races!

Over night, a white tent with red and yellow spires went up in a field downtown. The Webber Bros. Circus had come to town. Memories of when Circus Man visited Walnut Grove in *Little House on the Prairie* came to mind. His wagon was decorated in an advertisement "The Great O'Hara's Circus and Menagerie." Laura exclaimed, "Isn't that pretty." and Mary replied back "Just grand." They stood there in their pink and green dresses with bonnets hanging down their backs, eyes wide and smiles of anticipation on their faces. The same buzz and excitement was in the air in Wairoa.

I bought tickets for Elena and myself, then we found our seats. We were dazzled with a more European style circus. Trapeze artists flew into one another's arms far above our heads. Clowns made us laugh until our sides hurt. Women balanced on the backs of prancing horses. I left with the young, carefree feeling that only the circus can bring.

Then one day, without warning, an eclectic mix of portable homes moved into a field. Wooden houses built on the frames of old trucks were painted bright colors. Lace curtains hung in windows. People unloaded tables and chairs to set up camp in the middle of town. The gypsies had arrived.

Young thin women with long hair cascading down their backs and old fat women with silver streaks in hair wound into buns looked out of windows or peered out of doors. As they stepped out of their portable homes, brightly colored toenails peeked out from under their long, full peasant skirts made of velvet and brocade. A shawl covered the shoulders of their ruffled blouses and bangles tinkled in the air as they waved their hand to a friend in greeting. Large gold earrings swung with their hair and multiple necklaces hung around their necks, sparkling in the sunlight. A few of the more modern girls had nose and lip piercings, which just added to the Bohemian effect. Painted signs hung from the campers luring the curious in for palm readings and tarot card foretelling. Others sold homemade hemp jewelry, silver rings or did hair braiding. Men added their offerings to the mix with homemade shoes, wooden chairs and tattooing services.

Lest one think that New Zealand is overrun with gypsies, I learned that this group was more like a club. They held normal jobs during the day and traveled on the weekends to meet up with friends and live in community for a few days.

Family Visits

Whether separated by a few small towns or by continents and oceans, when family is not close at hand, friends become family. Lives intermix. Holidays are spent together. Vacations knit the relationships tight. The lives of friends' children become as important as if they were nieces and nephews. But magic happens in our souls when family comes to visit. Conversations on the phone or Skype are understood after a visit. A deeper bond is created because a great distance was crossed and sacrifice was made to be together. Time together is no longer taken for granted, rather it is cherished and valued.

For months we had been anticipating the summer visit of my parents. When days got a bit rough and lonely I would dream of seeing my folks and sharing with them all of the wonderful places and people that I had come to love. When my parents stepped off the plane in Auckland, walked through the gate and into my open arms, it was a reunion fit for a soldier returning from war. A flurry of hugs and kisses amongst comments of "My how you have grown." echoed through the airport.

Although we did a whirlwind tour of the North Island, the times that I hold dear in my heart are the days spent in our little town of Wairoa. We shared meals and introduced our new extended family. We walked the streets of our town, ate fish and chips by the river, and played with Moko the dolphin in the bay. Later when I would speak on the phone with my mom and tell her I had just walked home from Elena's school, she could imagine me walking through the alley painted in colorful graffiti on the corrugated metal walls with flaming pink bougainvillea creeping over the fence. If I said I was in the kitchen, she could envision me standing on the well-worn linoleum flooring while stirring a pot on the burner next to the little wood burning stove with its white chimney pipe reaching up to the ceiling. A new understanding grew between us. They began to understand this vagabond life we had chosen.

We spent a magical day on the beach when some friends invited us to their bach in Mahia. Chad went for a dive. He brought back a good catch of lobster. Our hosts boiled it and we ate slowly, savoring the freshness, just moments out of the ocean. We walked on the reef discovering some new creatures hidden in the tidal pools. We looked through binoculars, glimpsing orca whales swimming out near the horizon. Memories were woven into our hearts as we breathed the same fresh salty air and walked in one another's footprints on the beach. I knew we would pull them out to recall on a gloomy day when we were once again separated by distance.

The most precious memory was the Sunday morning that we sat on the patio nibbling on fresh cinnamon buns dripping with white, creamy icing. I sipped a homemade mocha thick with the sweet flavor of chocolate sauce and drank in the scent of the blooming wisteria dangling on the trellis overhead. Around the cheap glass table, my parents shared their spiritual journey. My dad recalled attending church as a young man, being involved then realizing that it was just empty good deeds and something needed to break in his heart. He told us of talking to God and spilling it all out in confession and repentance to Him. He recalled small changes that began to happen deep within the very core of his soul. My mom talked of the faithfulness of her parents' devotion to God in humble circumstances and the choice she made to live with the same convictions that they had taken into their lives.

For me, New Zealand was a place of deep soul searching. Of finding God outside the walls of a church. Knowing that He was deep within me because I had asked Him to be there. The relationship that I had with the God I believed in while I lived my life in the comfort of middle-class America and attended church on Sundays needed to be strong enough to carry me when there were no friends or family and no church building to sit in or pastor to tell me how to follow God.

One Sunday morning in a tiny little town, three generations sat together, speaking and listening to one another. We need to share our hearts and souls with those we love. I need to tell my children why God is important to me.

Three weeks passed in a blur as if it were a racecar zipping by in a flurry of color. Elena and I took my parents on one last wild ride through the mountains to the airport. Elena said "goodbye." When she turned to leave, the tears began to trickle down her cheeks. I picked her up and nestled her face in the crook of my neck. My arms held tight as her little body shook with emotion and I felt moisture slipping down my face as well. I carried her quietly to the car. I realized a little part of each of us had flown away on that plane with my parents, but the greater part was still alive and active in New Zealand, continuing in the adventure.

The Bach

One holiday weekend Ruth and Russell invited us to spend the night with some of their friends in "The Hut." The "hut" being referring to was the bach located on a friend's station.

As we had been learning throughout the year, the term "bach" was simply a holiday or weekend home. In Michigan when someone spoke of their holiday home they were talking about their condo in Florida or a cottage up north on a lake. White painted picket fences, flower gardens and a welcome mat by the front door greet visitors. They are nice cozy spots where one goes to leave the city behind.

In New Zealand, a bach typically refers to a post World War II shack constructed of whatever materials were available. These vacation homes became highly popular in the 50's and it is speculated that the term was simply short for "bachelor pad," even though typically they were family holiday homes. As families vacationed every year at the same spot on the beach, these homes began popping up. Recently, high-class holiday homes on the beach for the wealthy are becoming more popular and are being referred to as baches as well.

We packed our stuff knowing it would be a bit of a camping experience and followed Ruth and Russell out to the farm, thirty minutes away. It drizzled as we pulled into the driveway where we transferred all our stuff into the back of Russell's Ute. The last thing to go into the back before driving off were the kids. They squeezed in—four faces staring out with chins resting on their knees. We headed out over the farm, not following a road, but just driving in a general direction, through gates and pastures and wooded areas. Absolutely beautiful!

Russell pulled up to a couple more trucks and parked. We had planned to ride four-wheelers the rest of the way into the bach, but because of recent rain we would have to hike. He was prepared, handing each of us a pair of gumboots to wear for the weekend. We headed off into the woods down a very, very long hill. From the car I often admired the hills, wistfully saying "wouldn't it be fun to climb one?" The next morning would fulfill all my desires for a lifetime to come. We slipped and slid down the hill on a two-track road. Thick forest surrounded us. Tall deciduous trees mixed with tree ferns, grasses and vines created a wild jungle to lose ourselves in for the weekend. Just around a curve "The Hut" came into view.

Situated amongst the trees, a corrugated metal building with a rickety looking porch and new awning welcomed us. Streaks of red paint on the metal sides revealed how patched together with scraps our weekend retreat was. Smoke drifted out of a metal chimney, hinting at a warm and cozy interior. We trudged up carrying our gear, our feet heavy with thick mud, and were greeted by two other families. After throwing our bags inside and tossing our sleeping bags on the bed we grabbed a chair and settled on the porch for an evening of visiting.

My stomach growled at the scent of sausages and venison steaks on the grill—nothing fancy, just a metal box with fire underneath the solid metal sheet to fry the meat on. The hike had left me famished. I was reminded how good camp food was as I held a warm sausage in a bun. We talked and laughed with new friends while the rain became more intense and the temperature began to drop. I rubbed my hands together and shivered a bit. We decided to head inside.

At that moment we discovered that everyone was outside the bach and the door was locked. A thirty minute comedy of hemming and hawing, walking around The Hut and going back and forth with different lengths of wood and other things ensued. Eventually the men were able to pry a window partly open and lower Elena through. Everyone breathed a sigh of relief as we dismissed thoughts of spending the night in the rainy, dark jungle.

The bach consisted of one rectangular room. The walls were simply the other side of the corrugated metal. Reclaimed 2x4s provided a framework for the structure. An "L" of plywood cabinets painted brown with white knobs lined a corner. Bright orange Formica countertops were laden with the potluck of food everyone had contributed. Two large windows provided natural lighting for the room. A hose snaked from two gas burners to a propane tank on the floor.

The kids sat in various lawn chairs around a wood table. A game of cards was in session. A cry would burst out each time a knuckle was rapped with a spoon. Laughter filled the bach as the night wore on. A wood-burning stove was tucked into another corner, keeping the room nice and toasty. The customary rope was strung above the stove with all manner of wet clothing draped over it. The slight smell of damp wool socks permeated the room. A patchwork of carpet scraps covered the floor. Chad was sunk deep into an old couch next to the stove talking with the men.

It didn't take me long to realize that there was no toilet in the rectangle room. A trip outside to the "long-drop" meant facing the cold and rain. I put on my gumboots and made a run for it in the moonless night with only a torch to light the way.

When I came back into the room, an open bag of marshmallows sat on the table. Kiwis are not familiar with 'smores, but one family had heard of them so they brought the fixings to experiment with. New Zealand marshmallows are not the same as American marshmallows. They are small, pink teardrops sprinkled with powdered sugar, and a bit on the grainy side of things. After unsuccessfully trying to explain the concept of roasting rather than burning the marshmallows, we put them on cookies. Again, there are no graham crackers in New Zealand. I searched high and low and nobody had heard of them so we used chocolate-coated cookies instead. From an American perspective it was a sad, feeble attempt. But from the teens' perspective they were triumphant in this exotic treat. I kept my thoughts to myself as we prepared for bed. I was happy we got to share a bit of our homeland traditions with our new friends.

One entire wall was dedicated to the bunk bed. A twelve-foot long and six foot deep frame held mattresses lined up next to each other. An old wooden ladder was propped against the top bunk. One at a time, the eight kids climbed the ladder and spread out their sleeping bags. Soon they had formed a circle up there, sitting Indian style, playing another game of cards.

That left the bottom bunk for the eight adults. My mind worked through ways to get into my sleeping bag and lay flat without kicking anyone in the back. Like sardines packed tightly in a tin, I stayed stiff as a board—Chad on one side and Russell on the other. I was terrified to move, thinking I might snuggle with the wrong man. Eventually I fell asleep, grateful that no one in the group snored.

I awoke fresh. It was still drizzling, but after a trip to the long drop I headed out for a bit of an explore. As I walked along a beautiful path, I came across a river with several fabulous swimming holes. What a place to relax on a sunny day! After breakfast and dishes were done, we packed and headed back up the hill. It was long, steep and slippery but we made it without loosing anything.

Hanging out with friends in a place with minimum amenities was one of the best New Zealand experiences we had.

The South Island

Because we lived on the North Island, the majority of our time was spent there. We were only able to take one week to experience as much of the South Island as possible. That small amount of time only whetted my appetite to return in the future.

As we flew over Cook Strait, which unites the Tasman Sea to the Pacific Ocean, I immediately saw a topographical difference between the two islands. The North Island is covered with small, green, hilly mountains where thick and lush forests of deciduous trees mingle with palms. The tallest mountain and active volcano, Mt. Raupehu, rises to 9,176 feet. In contrast, the South Island has the tall and rugged Southern Alps running down its backbone with Mt. Cook rising to 12,316 feet. Rivers and fiords crisscross the island. The difference in longitude as New Zealand reaches for Antarctica kisses away the mild climate.

The South Island is the larger of the two islands and is the twelfth largest island in the world. The Maori have two names for the island; *Te Waka a Maui,* calling the island "the canoe that Maui used to fish the North Island out of the sea," and *Te Wai Pounamu* meaning "The Waters of Greenstone." The small population of the island and the ruggedness give it a feeling of a pioneer frontier land.

Greymouth

The largest town on the South Island's west coast is Greymouth, named for the mouth of the Grey River where the city is located. Not grey in color, the river was named in 1848 by explorer Thomas Brunner in honor of the Governor of New Zealand, Sir George Grey. The river is still often called *Mawhere,* the Maori name meaning "wide spread river mouth." Gold and coal mining brought Europeans to the area, and when the mining industry began to decline, forestry and fishing became more important.

Greymouth is one of the few locations in the world where Katabatic winds sweep high density air down the mountains under the force of gravity. Winds can reach hurricane speeds, although most are not that intense. Locally these winds are called "The Barber," sweeping into the area with a coldness and mist that bites to the bone. You can often see the front as it sweeps over the mountains into the city.

The most spectacular way to arrive in Greymouth is via the TranzAlpine railroad. KiwiRail Scenic Journeys offers three rail lines throughout the country. The Northern Explorer travels between Wellington and Auckland right through the heart of the North Island. It passes through farmland, native forests, over river gorges and across a volcanic plateau. You will believe you are in the land of the Hobbits. The Coastal Pacific line begins in Picton where you can walk from the ferry terminal to the train station. The journey to Christchurch travels along sixty miles of rugged coastline with the surging Pacific Ocean viewed through one window and the steep Kaikoura Ranges on the other side. The train passes through the wine growing region of Blenheim and the farmland of the Canterbury Plains.

The four and a half hour journey from Christchurch to Greymouth on the TranzAlpine line is considered one of the world's most scenic train trips.

Excited for a South Island adventure, Maddie and I boarded the silver and blue train in Christchurch, found our seats and snuggled up for the long ride. As the train chugged through the mountains, the leaves on the trees sparkled their brilliant hues of red, orange and yellow. Warm and cozy inside the car, we watched out the large window as the world flew past. Maddie laid her head on my shoulder. She breathed a sigh of deep contentment. We both felt the peace of the moment. We were far away from life where nothing could touch us. I didn't have to think about finding a job in a few months when I returned home. I had no worries of packing and moving. Maddie didn't have to face the idea of saying "goodbye" to friends or her cat. It was a day when we could just be mom and daughter sharing a special moment that we could remember forever, no matter how far away we were.

Fall was a good time to see the Southern Alps in all their colorful glory. We followed along a river, then passed through thick brush and streamed through tunnels carved deep in the mountain. High above deep gorges we got dizzy looking at jagged rocks and careening water. Snow covered mountains loomed in the distance. We gazed, read, chatted and relaxed during our journey to Greymouth.

The weather changed from pleasant to windy and rainy when we crossed to the western side of the mountains. We only had a short hour to grab some lunch at a diner before re-boarding for the trip home. We snuggled in for the four-hour return trip, pleased with the getaway this day had provided for us.

The local brewery, **Monteith's**, is a bit of a New Zealand legend. They run tours and offer tasting sessions. Established in 1868, they create distinctive beers which earn them the reputation of being the leader of the craft beer market in New Zealand.
Cnr Turumaha & Herbert Streets
www.monteiths.co.nz

Shantytown was built to be a recreation of a nineteenth century gold rush town. It offers steam train rides and gold panning. It is located 11 km south of Greymouth. The town takes you back in time to the early days of New Zealand.
Rutherglen Rd.
Paoroa
www.shantytown.co.nz

TranzAlpine Railroad
http://www.kiwirailscenic.co.nz

Mount Cook

Legend of the Ngai Tahu (the local Maori people) says that the young son of Rakinui (the Sky Father) named Aoraki, along with his three brothers took a voyage around Papatuanuku (the Earth Mother) in a canoe. Disaster struck and they became stranded on a reef in Aoraki's canoe named *Te Waka a Aoraki*. When the boat tilted to one side, Aoraki and his brothers climbed to the top of the wreck and sat down to wait. A strong wind blew in from the south and froze them into stone. The South Island, stretched long like the canoe, used to be called *Te Waka o Aoraki*, reminding all Maori how this land came to be. Aoraki, the tallest of the brothers, froze into Mount Cook while the other brothers became smaller peaks in the mountain range. This is the story of the Southern Alps or *Ka Tiritiri ore Moana*.

As Christchurch was waking up, Damon and I wandered down the street from the hotel and found a coffee shop open for breakfast before boarding a tour bus that would take us on an excursion to Aoraki/Mount Cook National Park. I was excited to spend this day with my son exploring another small slice of New Zealand together. We took our seats while the guide began weaving stories filled with legends, facts and songs.

We stopped for a mid-way break to stretch our legs and wander around Lake Tekapo. The brilliant turquoise waters pulled us to the rocky edge. The sun sparkled on small waves dancing in the breeze of New Zealand's highest large lake. The unique effect of the turquoise water is created by "rock flour." Rocks are ground into fine dust particles by the glaciers then suspended in the water. The sunlight bouncing off the particles into the glacial melt-waters gives a blue-green hue to the lake.

Snow capped mountains rose in the distance. This was the ideal spot for a stone church. The *Church of the Good Shepherd* was built in 1935 as a memorial to the pioneers of the area. No sermon needs to be preached to those sitting in the pews of this tiny church, for the view of Lake Takapo and the white-capped mountains through the altar window speak in awe of God's creation.

A land of hard ice and rock composes the terrain of the two hundred seventy square mile park. Glaciers, which cover forty percent of the land, have helped to carve out five major valley systems and the nineteen sharp peaks that dominate the sky.

The Tasman glacier is New Zealand's largest and longest glacier. It covers thirty-nine square miles, stretching to two and one half miles at its widest point. It's an astounding two thousand feet thick yet it's retreating five hundred ninety feet each year. Scientist believe that due to climate change we will loose Tasman glacier in approximately one hundred to two hundred years along with many other glaciers across the country. We were thrilled to catch a glimpse of it from the highway as we headed into the park.

We didn't have time to take advantage of some of the walking paths near the visitor's center, but we did enjoy a leisurely lunch at the Sir Edmund Hillary Cafe & Bar. Lazy like the clouds drifting past Aoraki/Mount Cook, we munched on sandwiches and soaked in the afternoon sun.

The highest peak in New Zealand, Aoraki/Mount Cook rises 12,316 feet into the blue sky. In 1998 the peak was renamed Aoraki/Mount Cook to recognize its Maori history. Aoraki/Mount Cook is the only name in New Zealand where the Maori name precedes the English name. On a sunny day, her distinct, snow capped rock face can be seen while sitting on the deck of the visitor's center. Her rugged peak slices into the clouds, beckoning the wildly adventurous. She is not a stroll in the park on a sunny afternoon, but rather a strenuous, albeit moderately technical sixteen to twenty-two hour climb. People from far and wide have been attracted to what is known as one of the finest mountaineering areas of the world. Aoraki/Mount Cook was first summited by the New Zealand trio of Tom Fyfe, Jack Clarke and George Graham on Christmas Day in 1894. Others had been trying to succeed for twelve years. Local outfitters know how to read the weather in the area and what entries are best if you wish to try it yourself.

We wandered into the Sir Edmund Hillary Alpine Centre, looked at the exhibits and watched a documentary. Each nation has its heroes and Sir Edmund Hillary is a name that reaches far beyond the boarders of this small, remote nation and into homes around the world. "The first man to summit Mount Everest" began his life in 1919 in Auckland. He grew up attending school and helping his father in the beekeeping business. A passion for reading adventure stories soon turned into pursuing adventures of his own.

In 1935 Hillary traveled with his school to ski on Mount Ruapehu. He fell in love with the mountains and began skiing, hiking and eventually climbing whenever he could manage time away. Mount Oliver was the first mountain he climbed a few years later.

During WWII, Hillary enlisted with the Royal New Zealand Air Force. He was injured in battle while serving as a navigator. He returned home determined to conquer his injuries and to continue to conquer mountains.

Hillary resumed his climbing in New Zealand, favoring the Southern Alps. He made his first ascent of Aoraki/Mount Cook in 1948 and today the south ridge has been renamed *Hillary Ridge* in honor of his life. He built a solid reputation and began climbing in Europe. He was invited by Sir John Hunt to join an expedition preparing to climb Mount Everest. Hilary trained with Hunt in the Scottish Highlands for two years before they joined twenty of the best climbers in the world at Everest. Never before had anyone successfully summited Mount Everest. On May 29, 1953, Hillary and his Nepalese climbing partner, Tenzing Norgay, were the last two in their party able to attempt the summit. At 11:30 a.m. they reached the highest spot on earth. Hillary continued to pursue exploration in his life, eventually turning from exploring the earth to exploring the needs of mankind. His eyes remained focused on the Nepalese people and

New Zealand. He never stopped working to help create a better world for both countries.

Due to the nature of group touring we hustled back to the bus for the return journey to Christchurch. Just as the scenery was flying by my window, I knew the years would pass quickly and my son would grow into a man. I hope that a day spent with towering mountains and the stories of men who climbed them would inspire him to greatness in every effort he makes in life.

The Hermitage
Lodging, Dining, Sir Edmund Hillary Alpine Centre
www.hermitage.co.nz

Aoraki Mt Cook Visitor Centre
Mount Cook National Park DOC Visitor Centre Mount Cook
T 03-435-1186
www.mtcooknz.com

<u>Christchurch</u>

I think back to the few days we spent in Christchurch and realize that it's changed. Just as visitors walked the Silica Terraces of Rotorua one hundred thirty years ago, I walked the landscape of this city that is now changed by nature. Physical things, locked in my mind to be experienced over and over again, are gone.

I remember the day the earthquake struck in February 2011. It was one of those events that the world sat and watched in helpless horror. This one, a natural disaster. A violent earthquake measuring 6.3 rocked the city in the middle of the day. People were out on lunch break, visitors were enjoying the sites. The city was full of life and activity one moment, then two minutes later it was full of death and chaos. Offices collapsed, bricks fell from buildings, and busses crashed. One-hundred-eighty-five people were killed, and thousands injured. These two minutes devastated the tiny island nation.

I ran over to my computer and began frantically emailing those friends who had become so dear during the year. Many of them had family in Christchurch. Instant communication is a love/hate relationship for me. Through Facebook, Twitter and TV, I know about news happening around the world within moments. The horror of disaster, war and terrorism is in my face and I must deal with it while trying to comprehend how something so far away is suddenly sitting with me in my living room. On the other hand, I was able to immediately tell my friends that I was thinking about them, that I was on my knees praying for their families.

The earthquake that day changed the third largest city in New Zealand forever. As life is often measured in terms of what happened before or after a major, life-changing event, my memories are from before the quake. I know I can never return to experience the same things, they are frozen in my memory.

My first impression of the South Island was the distinct difference in feel from the North Island. English. Only ten percent of the Maori people live on the South Island, so the Maori culture that shapes so much of the North Island and particularly the area where we were living, is absent. The first Europeans landed in the Canterbury area in 1815. They began to settle the land in 1840 and by 1850 whaling operations were running out of Lyttelton. In 1850 and 1851 the first settlers who founded Christchurch arrived on the "first four ships." Christchurch became the first city by Royal Charter, which makes it the oldest city in New Zealand.

Christchurch made New Zealand known in 1893 when it granted women the right to vote—a first in the world. Kate Sheppard started the New Zealand Women's Christian Temperance Union. The group realized it would be much easier to achieve reforms if women had the right to vote. Her home in Christchurch became a regular meeting place for suffrage campaigners which eventually swung Parliament in their favor. Upon her death in 1934, the *Christchurch Times reported:* "A great woman has gone, whose name will remain an inspiration to the daughters of New Zealand while our history endures."

Voted number two on the list of "52 Places to Go in 2014" by *The New York Times*, Christchurch and the surrounding area have much to offer. Outdoor activities from skiing, hiking and mountain biking, to water sports like rafting, surfing and swimming, to cultural places like gardens and wineries are all close at hand. Nature and wildlife are abundant in the mountains and sea.

Expansive parks provide sanctuary for the weary soul and give an overall feeling of leisure to the town known as the "Garden City." The heart of the city can be found in the Botanic Gardens. Nestled in a loop of the Avon River and bordered on three sides by Hagley Park, the gardens are one of the city's most popular attractions. We strolled under the tall, old trees, through the rolling green grass and along the river, crossing back and forth on the many bridges.

The punters dressed in smart white shirts with suspenders, vests and ties. Their boaters, or straw hats, shaded them from the midday sun. They stood at the end of the flat-bottomed boats, pushing them lazily down the river with a long pole. Couples snuggled romantically in the bottom while children hung over the edge splashing passing ducks. There wasn't a better way to spend a fresh fall afternoon than strolling around, enjoying the peacefulness of trees draping their branches over the river and beds of flowers with their colorful faces turned to the sun.

If winter is a novel idea to you, be sure to visit the International Antarctic Centre. Here one can learn about the impact humans have had on the Antarctic continent. Discover a land that is ninety-eight percent covered by ice—the coldest, driest and windiest place on the earth. Have fun experiencing a simulated snowstorm, ride in the Hagglund and observe the Little Blue Penguins.

Cathedral Square, in the center of the city, received major impact during the earthquake. When we visited, we wandered from our hotel into the lively and vibrant square. Street entertainers kept us fascinated while we munched on goodies from vendors. Christchurch Cathedral was magnificent. Built of local stone, the cathedral was completed in the second half of the nineteenth century. The spire, which fell in the quake, rose two hundred seven feet above the square, consistent with the Gothic Revival style. My little girls looked in awe at the high arches made of stone. Tall, thin stained glass windows let slivers of light in to dance on the floor. The grand rose window was similar to rose windows in the great Gothic cathedrals of Europe. Today the Anglican church building has been decommissioned. While they are deciding if they will tear down or repair the original church, the community is worshiping at the Cardboard Cathedral. When I first heard that they were constructing a building, of any sort, out of cardboard I laughed. All I could imagine were the paths and houses I had built out of toilet paper tubes for our pet hamsters. As their website claims, "It will be the world's only cathedral made substantially of cardboard." The new cathedral, opened August 2013, is a five-minute walk from the ruins of the old, and located at the southern end of Latimer Square. Japanese disaster architect Shigeru Ban designed the seven hundred seat cathedral with construction materials from twenty-four inch diameter cardboard tubes to timber beams, structural steel and concrete. Much of the building materials were sourced locally and nationally. Its A-fame style rises seventy-eight feet in height. Even many pieces of furniture appear to be constructed out of cardboard tubes. The focal point is the amazing triangular glass window. Rather that replicate the original rose window, the designer created a triangle window comprised of forty-nine panels nearly four feet long. Identical images and placements from the original window were incorporated into the new triangle window. High-resolution photographs of the original window were printed on glass panels and fired in a kiln.

Four years have passed since the fateful earthquake. Christchurch is still in the process of redefining itself. Decisions are still being made on what to keep and what to demolish. The vision is to move the city in a greener and safer direction. Rebirth takes time, but with publications such as *The New York Times* and *Tripadvisor* encouraging tourism, the city has hope and is shining in a new, vibrant way.

Botanic Gardens
http://www.ccc.govt.nz/cityleisure/parkswalkways/christchurchbotanicgardens/index.aspx

Christchurch Punting on the Avon
www.punting.co.nz

Cardboard Cathedral
234 Hereford St.
http://www.cardboardcathedral.org.nz
Virtual tour

International Antarctic Centre
38 Orchard Road
Christchurch Airport
www.iceberg.co.nz

Akaroa

The quaint little historic French village of Akaroa, just fifty miles from Christchurch, made a nice mini destination. At this point, driving on the left hand side of the road was second nature, so we rented a car to give ourselves some freedom.

We stopped several times along the way just so I could take out my camera and breathe in the beautiful scenery. Nine months in this country and I still had not gotten over the cuteness of sheep grazing on rolling hills, or a colonial stone church with a colorful door nestled amongst a grove of trees.

A stop at Barry's Cheese was an excuse for some education in the fine art of making cheese. Opened in 1895, they are the only factory left on the peninsula that still makes their cheese in the traditional method. We enjoyed watching the rhythmic process of men dragging a frame through the vats of dairy and stirring the curdles to create the cheese. We wandered around the store, nibbling on every sample before choosing our purchases. Once again New Zealand had offered us the opportunity to see things from start to finish. The cows grazing in the fields with little calves by their side to a block of cheese in a bag ready for our lunch.

Over a hill and around a corner the valley opened before us giving us our first glimpse of the bay. Dark green trees sat in clumps on a carpet of brilliant green grass that rose and fell over the hills, then slid into the sparkling blue waters of the bay. Puffy white clouds reflected in the water. There are no words to describe a view so beautiful and peaceful.

Downtown offered a nice variety of shops, French bakeries and cafes to spend a leisurely afternoon in. It was a bit past the season of outside dining, so we enjoyed gazing out windows at the pine trees surrounding the bay. Sailboats dotted the water while distant memories of summer lingered in the air.

Our little kids needed to see some little animals. Akaroa Bay is home to the Hector's Dolphin and the White Flippered Penguin; both are some of the smallest in their species.

The Hector's Dolphin is named after Sir James Hector, a New Zealand zoologist who first collected the species in 1869. This small grey dolphin has a white tummy with a pretty white flame that comes up along its side. His face, flippers, fin and tail are black. This little guy is only about three and a half to four and a half feet long and weighs up to one hundred ten pounds—tiny compared to Moko the seven foot Bottlenose that we were used to playing with. A discriminating feature of a Hector's Dolphin is the round dorsal fin that looks a bit like a Mickey Mouse ear. Their snout is rounded giving it the appearance of a beak. Their cousins, the Maui's Dolphin (North Island Hector's Dolphin), are the rarest dolphins on earth. So the South Island Hector's Dolphin is the second rarest dolphin in the world. There are less than eight thousand left. They are all concentrated in the Christchurch area and are an endangered species. Playful pods of five or six dolphins ran along with our boat for bits of time. The kids loved standing at the rail watching their games. I felt so lucky that we were able to see this rare, little gem.

The White Flippered Penguin is another tiny animal that is found specifically around the Christchurch area. They are only about one foot tall and weigh three pounds. Like all penguins, they have white bellies, but they find their distinction in white markings on their flippers. They are nocturnal birds, but we were lucky to have one little penguin swim along with us. Like a bullet he would skim through the water then resurface further ahead. It was a bit hard to see him because he was so small and his lightning movement made it a game to track where he was.

Further up the coast we came across a colony of New Zealand Fur Seals. This common seal can be seen all over the shores of the country. The black volcanic rock was covered with lazy seals warming in the sun. They poked their pointy noses into the air to let us know that they knew we were near. These animals are massive, funny creatures. They looked harmless from the safety of the boat, but I would not want to meet one of these five hundred and fifty pounds of pure muscle up close and personal.

The boat turned around to slowly make its way back to the harbor. The winds hit us head-on. We used our coats to make parachutes that held us upright when we leaned. We were not alone in our antics. Everyone on board was laughing at this circus the wind was providing. Suddenly a huge bird flew over the boat. We all turned to look. In that moment the kids knew that the "Rescue Aid Society" had convened and Orville, the albatross, had been called into duty. Penny must be saved. Miss Bianca, the mouse, settled into her sardine can of a seat. Her partner Bernard read the checklist to Orville:

Orville: Say, bud, read the checklist to me.
Bernard: Uh, oh, yeah. Goggles down.
Orville: [dons his goggles] Check.
Bernard: Wing flaps down.
Orville: Check.
Bernard: Tail feathers.
Orville: Double check.
Bernard: If at first you don't succeed, try, try again.
Orville: [takes off] And here we go!

Orville lumbered down the deck. His large feet padded on the wooden runway and he panted heavily in an attempt to lift into the sky. Bernard hung on tight and Miss Bianca smiled in glee. Coming to the end of the runway the great albatross dove, nose first off the top of the skyscraper leaving a trail of feathers behind.

Miss Bianca: Ohhh. I just love "takeoffs."[11]

I had never seen an albatross before, and my only association was Walt Disney's depiction in *The Rescuers*. The albatross is the largest seabird. Like me, they are travelers at heart and can fly one hundred twenty thousand miles in a year. Sometimes they travel ten thousand miles just to deliver a meal to their chicks as they wander between breeding grounds and search for food. They only use land for breeding, spending the rest of their lives journeying the ocean. The largest of the albatross have wingspans up to eleven feet, longer than any other bird. Fourteen varieties of albatross can be found in the Akaroa bay area. These funny, slightly uncoordinated birds were fun to watch. They would run across the sea, flapping their wings trying to get enough speed to lift off. Just as in the movie, I could hear their feet slapping against the water and their wings thumping in the air.

It was a privilege to experience new animals in their home, but we were ready to return home ourselves and knew the end of this great adventure was just a short time off.

Akaroa i-SITE Visitor Centre
120 Rue Jolie
akaroa@christchurchnz.com
03-304-8600

Barry's Bay Cheese
Located on highway 75 between Christchurch and Akaroa
http://www.barrysbaycheese.co.nz/visit-us.aspx

Akaroa Banks Peninsula Track
2-4 day hike
http://www.bankstrack.co.nz/index.html

Poha Tu Plunge
Guided tours to the protected Australasian Little Penguin colony
http://www.pohatu.co.nz/home.wse

Black Cat Cruises
Akaroa Harbour Nature Cruises
http://www.blackcat.co.nz/akaroa-harbour-nature-cruises.html

Saying "Goodbye"

Things were changing. I walked passed Stew's house and saw a "For Sale" sign pounded into his beautifully manicured lawn. My mind understood his need to move to his son's farm but my heart longed for life to go on without any changes. Ruth and Russell were going to be moving to the South Island in a few short weeks. Nothing in life is static; babies are born bringing joy and filling holes left by those who have gone before them.

King Solomon and the Byrds remind me that there is a season for everything under the sun.

There is a time for everything,
and a season for every activity under the heavens:
a time to be born and a time to die,

I had watched my friend's tummy grow large with child. A smile filled my face as I snuggled the wee bundle in my arms, thankful for the new life given to her.

Tears streamed down my face as Stew told me over our fence that Val had passed away. My heart ached over the loss of this special friend.

a time to plant and a time to uproot,

Eager to learn the fine art of gardening, I cradled the precious seedlings in my hands as Stew gently placed the plants in their holes and softly patted the earth around them.

I harvested the fruits and vegetables with pride, slaved over cookbooks to learn new recipes, then with hot-mitt covered hands, I laid our bounty before my family and friends.

a time to kill and a time to heal,

I watched my children with eyes so bright run and jump with the little lambs in our back yard. Chad took the lambs and killed them to provide meat for our family. The skins that now lay on the back of my chairs are a daily reminder of the sacrifice an animal made for my existence.

a time to tear down and a time to build,

I burned a hole in the carpet trying to learn how take care of a fire. One day the owner knocked on the door and announced that it was time to replace the carpet. I often looked down at my feet and was thankful for the newness and cleanness in contrast to the outdated wallpaper, cabinets and countertops. The house was so hard for me at first, but over time I saw my heart change as I focused less and less on the walls around me and more and more on the memories made within.

a time to weep and a time to laugh,
We shared moments with friends who had become close like family. When the tears streaked down our faces they cleansed our hearts and opened new spaces for joy. We laughed together over meals, on adventures and in one another's homes, creating memories that built our friendships strong for when the days of sorrow would come once again.

a time to mourn and a time to dance,
Floating in my mind, but stumbling in reality I learned that the art of dancing goes beyond the dance floor, deep into the soul of your partner.

a time to scatter stones and a time to gather them,
a time to embrace and a time to refrain from embracing,
a time to search and a time to give up,
Panic and fear wrapped their long fingers around my heart as I tried to descend into a wetta-filled cave with a group of elementary students. I clawed my way out, mindless of little children around me, and ran. By the time I found my way to the parking lot a search party had convened. I'm so thankful that they were not given a chance to "give up," loosing me forever to the wilds of New Zealand!

a time to keep and a time to throw away,
When this adventure began, we made a conscious decision to part with many of our earthly possessions. It was hard, I rather liked my stuff. But in the process of letting go of so many things, room was made in my heart for people. Things that wear out and are time-consuming were replaced with relationships that will last a lifetime.

a time to tear and a time to mend,
a time to be silent and a time to speak,
a time to love and a time to hate,
a time for war and a time for peace.
Ecclesiastes 3:1-8[12]

I wasn't prepared for the deep love I had for my new friends and this country that had been silently growing in my heart. It crept up unexpectedly, at the end making me want to hold onto every last moment possible. I am a different person; my days in New Zealand changed me. I now hang some of my clothes in the backyard to dry because they seem to last longer and smell fresher; I am more aware of my garbage and take great efforts in recycling. Changes have also happened deep inside my soul. The very core of who I was transformed like a butterfly slowly emerging from her cocoon. I look at the world differently, understanding there is more than one way to skin a cat. Experiences change us, but I know so many people who are too fearful to take the first steps of an adventure.

Our family bonded over the year in a way I never dreamed possible. We lived in a small house and were forced to spend all our time in the same room. Feeding the fire throughout the winter breathed new life into our busy American family. We depended on one another to survive in a new culture. Each person became a vital part of the whole. We began doing puzzles together, playing little games and trying new things we never would have alone—often just to stave off the monotony of the one room syndrome where homework, crafts and work were done. We shared adventures together that we will talk about forever.

Clouds come in many shapes and sizes. Some are grey and pour rain down, while others are puffy, illuminated by the sun. But there is one cloud I will never forget... the Long White Cloud.

How You Can Do It Too

You may think it's not easy to pick up life and have an adventure in another country. I guess it depends on how badly you really want it. Over the years I have encountered many people who have weighed the cost and decided it was worth the risk to spend some time traveling and living overseas. Different types of travel provide different experiences and opportunities. Take some time to list what you want to get out of your experience. Do you simply want to tour the world, or do you want to have the time and opportunity to develop friendships with locals? Do you want to live in an American bubble and only venture out to see a cultural show or two, or do you want to learn the language, shop in the stores and markets and make friends with national neighbors? Here are a few thoughts on how I have seen different people experience the world.

Backpackers - In America we think of backpacking as something that interrupts one's educational and career path rather than being an experience of enrichment. As we talked with young people who were backpacking through New Zealand we were surprised to learn of the European concept of a "gap year." Between high school and college, young people are often encouraged to take a year and explore a portion of the world. The value in gaining a wider worldview is a beneficial attribute in the employee the student will someday become. Careful financial planning and budgeting are necessary to make such a year feasible, and teach irreplaceable life lessons. A backpacker tends to stay in the lowest cost accommodations possible like youth hostels. We've met backpackers along the way and invited them to stay in our home when they pass through our city. Several have taken us up on it and beautiful and lasting relationships were built when we opened our home and lives to them.

But backpacking isn't exclusively for the young. We became friends with a mid-life couple in New Zealand whose kids were grown. They planned and saved, found someone to run their business for them, then flew off to the other side of the world—South America—and backpacked through the continent. In some ways the experience was more meaningful for them because they had more to risk at that point in their lives.

http://www.hostels.com
https://www.couchsurfing.org

Mission or Volunteer Work - Often people who love adventure, distant lands and cultures also love people and have a deep concern for their needs. This is how we got our feet wet. We volunteered at a mission hospital in Africa for six weeks. The kids, then ages three months through four years, came along. It gave us a chance to experience a foreign culture and really think about how much time we wanted to spend overseas in the future. We experienced first hand some of the positives and some of the negatives of raising third culture kids, dealing with non-government agencies and cultural issues. Sometimes the love for people overrides the fear of travel. Traveling with a small group of people can give you the support you may need to face new cultures and different ways of doing things. A short-term trip is a great way to find out if a specific country or organization is right for you. Check with your church or a local charity to discover the opportunities available.

http://www.habitat.org/eurasia/get_involved/global_village

Vocation - Take what you already do and use it in another country. If you teach, recruiters are looking to fill needs in local schools for English-speaking countries. Teaching at an international school provides a competitive income and family support. Our friend Russell wanted to work in another country, so he figured out what countries his NZ pilot's license would be valid in, then began making contacts. Another friend who is an EMT found an international company for which he travels all over the world as the emergency technician with a team of scientists. Think outside the box, spend some time on the Internet, attend trade fairs and talk to people.

Teaching English as a Second Language - If you are looking for a way to live in a foreign country and work at the same time, there is a need for English teachers in many parts of the world. Don't think of this as a "cushy" job with little to no work and eons of free time. ESL/EFL teachers do the same work as other teachers. They prepare lesson plans, teach classes, grade papers and may add on some additional tutoring jobs to earn some extra cash. Gone are the days of little to no experience needed for the job. The more training you have, the more competitive you are and the better jobs you will land. Job boards simply post all jobs forwarded to them. Remember that you still need to do background work on schools you are interested in teaching with.

Global Tesol College
Teaching English as a Foreign Language classes are available online and/or in the classroom. Jobs are posted for students here as well.
http://globaltesol.com

Dave's ESL Cafe
A well-known site for job postings.
http://www.eslcafe.com

Total ESL
A well-known job posting board.
www.totalesl.com

Corporate move - When I was in second grade my friend's dad, who worked for Dow Corning, took a two year position in Wales. My friend and I wrote letters back and forth and I began to learn about cross-cultural living experiences as only ten-year-old girls can communicate! Your company may offer opportunities to move for one to three years overseas as part of their international plan. These jobs allow you to stay with your company, keep your home and basically put life on hold in America for a few years while you take your family overseas. Housing and transportation, as well as return trips home to the States and education for your children, are typically included. Check with your company to see what opportunities are available.

Locum Tenens - This is how we experienced New Zealand. Many people are not familiar with this term, but it is simply a person who fills the duties of another. It is primarily used in medical field. Doctors, nurses, physician's assistants, nurse practitioners and psychiatrists are needed around the world to work in underserved areas. Short-term and long-term positions are available. Talk to representatives at conferences, search the Internet and do your homework to be sure you are signing a fair contract.

Government - The foreign service has various opportunities for careers overseas. Assignments are typically two to three years. Specialties such as medicine, computers, and security are needed as well as political careers. You may be surprised what professional backgrounds are needed. They offer benefits such as housing, moving, education and family support with each placement.

http://www.state.gov/careers/
http://www.usaid.gov/careers

Military - "Be all that you can be!" The military offers a wide range of training and experience including opportunities to take your career overseas. This is a long-term commitment requiring that you to believe in what you are doing with all your heart. Recruiters will help you decide if this is the right choice for you.

Contract Companies - There are companies who contract with the military and embassies around the world. Opportunities such as technology, construction, maintenance, food services, engineering and many more are available.

PAE: https://www.pae.com
Brown & Root: http://www.kbr.com

About the Author

I was born in a mid-size town in Michigan—not too big and not too small. My parents still live in the house where I grew up. People often ask me "How can you leave your family and move around the world?" First, I attribute this to the stability I had growing up. Second, I am not alone on this journey. Together with my husband and kids, we explore the world. We have our own language, our own experiences. New Zealand was just the beginning.

I have a passion for people. I want to help where there is hurting, mend what is broken, and bring joy where there is sadness. I thought this would be easier to do overseas, in a world that needs hands to help. But I have actually found that it is harder. I don't speak the same language, some places are not open to aid and at times there is already enough help. Sometimes money is what is needed most. So I have chosen to donate 50% of my profits from this book to Women at Risk.

I used to volunteer at WAR when I lived in Michigan. Their mission is to "unite and educate women to create circles of protection and hope around at-risk women and children through culturally sensitive, value-added intervention projects." They work with women in the United States and around the world.

Women at Risk
http://warinternational.org

To follow Kristen and her family's adventures throughout the world visit
http://notinert.blogspot.com

To follow Kristen's ramblings visit
http://looksattheheart.blogspot.com

Notes

[1] Jean Batten, *Alone In the Sky* (Ramsbury, UK: Airlife Publishing Limited, 1987).

[2] Merriam-Webster, *The Merriam-Webster Dictionary* (Springfield, Massachusetts: Merriam-Webster Mass Market, 2004).

[3] James Cook, *Captain Cook's Journal During the First Voyage Round the World* (The Project Gutenberg EBook, www.gutenberg.org) Chapter 5.

[4] Kiwitourism, *Gisborne New Zealand,* http://www.kiwitourism.com/gisborne/gisborne-area-guide.html, (accessed October 2013).

[5] Lyrics by Charles Hart, excepts from *Music of the Night* (http://www.reallyuseful.com/about-us/the-really-useful-group/, The Really Useful Group, 1986).

[6] John McCrae, *In Flanders Fields and Other Poems* (G.P. Putnam's Sons, 1919).

[7] English Folk Verse, *The Fifth of November* (1970).

[8] Jay Livingston and Ray Evans, *Silver Bells* (Paramount Music Corp., 1951).

[9] Yvonne Morrison, *A Kiwi Night Before Christmas* (Scholastic New Zealand Limited, 2009).

[10] *Classic Christmas Cake* (New Zealand Women's Weekly, October 29, 2006).

[11] Walt Disney Productions, *The Rescuers* (Disney Enterprises Inc, 1978).

[12] Committee on Bible Translation, *New International Version* (Grand Rapids, Michigan: Zondervan and Biblica, Inc. 2011).

22845470R00088

Printed in Great Britain
by Amazon